The
Multiplication
Effect

NEXT
LEADERSHIP NETWORK

The *Multiplication* Effect

Building a

LEADERSHIP PIPELINE

That Solves Your Leadership Shortage

MAC LAKE

THOMAS NELSON
Since 1798

Published in Nashville, Tennessee, by Thomas Nelson. Thomas Nelson is a registered trademark of HarperCollins Christian Publishing, Inc.

Thomas Nelson titles may be purchased in bulk for educational, business, fund-raising, or sales promotional use. For information, please e-mail SpecialMarkets@ ThomasNelson.com.

Scripture quotations are from the Holy Bible, New International Version®, NIV®. Copyright © 1973, 1978, 1984, 2011 by Biblica, Inc.® Used by permission of Zondervan. All rights reserved worldwide. www.Zondervan.com. The "NIV" and "New International Version" are trademarks registered in the United States Patent and Trademark Office by Biblica, Inc.®

Any Internet addresses, phone numbers, or company or product information printed in this book are offered as a resource and are not intended in any way to be or to imply an endorsement by Thomas Nelson, nor does Thomas Nelson vouch for the existence, content, or services of these sites, phone numbers, companies, or products beyond the life of this book.

ISBN 978-1-4002-1627-7 (eBook)
ISBN 978-1-4002-1626-0 (TP)

Library of Congress Control Number:2019952446

Printed in the United States of America

HB 01.25.2024

About Leadership ✷ Network

Leadership Network fosters innovation movements that activate the church to greater impact. We help shape the conversations and practices of pacesetter churches in North America and around the world. The Leadership Network mind-set identifies church leaders with forward-thinking ideas—and helps them to catalyze those ideas resulting in movements that shape the church.

Together with HarperCollins Christian Publishing, the biggest name in Christian books, the NEXT imprint of Leadership Network moves ideas to implementation for leaders to take their ideas to form, substance, and reality. Placed in the hands of other church leaders, that reality begins spreading from one leader to the next . . . and to the next . . . and to the next, where that idea begins to flourish into a full-grown movement that creates a real, tangible impact in the world around it.

**NEXT: A Leadership Network Resource
committed to helping you grow your next idea.**

leadnet.org/NEXT

Contents

Content

PART 5: CONTENT

PART 6: PEOPLE

PART 7: OUTCOME

Foreword

Two decades ago I had the privilege of giving my full-time vocational energies to the role of "pastor of leadership development." It
was hard to find a peer in America with a similar title. Yet somehow
I found Mac Lake. I still remember our first conversation like it was
yesterday: I could not draw the strategic scribble on my Moleskine
journal page fast enough. On the one hand I found a peer, because
Mac was humble, approachable, and very kind to a fellow pastor in
the ranks. On the other hand I found a master, because my thinking
was uniquely challenged, my heart was unexpectedly lifted, and my
application was forever upgraded.

After getting to know Mac, even years later, I have never ques-
tioned the fact that God raised him up to be North America's most
influential leadership development coach for the church in our era.
The book you now hold is a true gift to God's people. It is the new
go-to book for any leader who has ever aspired to develop another
leader in the name of Jesus.

My claim is anchored in Mac's dynamic blend of experience,
passion, gifting, and commitment. Mac is a tireless trainer and bril-
liant toolmaker. He generously exhausts himself to serve the church
without compare, thus ensuring his ideas are as practical as they are
profound and as grounded as they are proven. From church planting
he went on to become the leadership pastor of one of America's original
gigachurches. He then invented a training process that impacts more
church planters today than any other leadership development system
in the United States. Finally, up close I have watched Mac deliver

break-through onsite consulting to install a leadership pipeline in existing churches, a process we continue to use at Auxano.

If that isn't impressive enough, Mac's personal modeling of what he teaches and his tenacious drive for improvement make him a mountain-like mentor amidst the vast variety of foothill experts.

But enough about Mac: let's talk about your culture of leadership development for a moment.

You have probably been convinced that to some degree "everything rises and falls on leadership." Yet the church today acts as if everything rises and falls on ministry programming this Sunday. I have never met a pastor who doesn't live with a deep hunch that something should be different or better as it pertains to multiplying disciples and training leaders.

Today we have no lack of life-changing teaching and melt-your-face worship in the best church buildings that money can buy. And Sunday after Sunday church continues. But some fruit that Jesus envisioned is conspicuously absent—an abundant harvest of reproducing leaders (as Mac is fond of saying).

Mac has permanently removed "I don't know how" from among the possible excuses for not multiplying more leaders in your church.

May this powerful and accessible playbook lift the trajectory of your ministry for the rest of your life. May your legacy reflect a parade of ongoing people development rather than a flash of programatic charisma.

> Will Mancini, founder of Auxano and Younique, author of *God Dreams*

Introduction

It's a moment that changed my story forever.

In many ways, there was nothing unique about the day. The average person watching me walk around Dallas Theological Seminary (DTS) on this fall afternoon would not have known the intense work God was doing in my soul.

It had been fifteen years since I'd left DTS. I came to campus an inexperienced leader with a passion for God and deep respect for Dr. Howard Hendricks. His unique blend of challenge, inspiration, and practical application prompted admiration for his work, and I took every class I could under him. All these years later, after practicing the principles I learned as Leadership Development Pastor at Seacoast Church in Mt. Pleasant, South Carolina, I had returned to the Dallas area with our staff for a conference.

One afternoon I snuck off to spend some time at the DTS campus and drifted into the chapel for some quiet time to reflect and thank God for His kindness in my life during the season I spent there. God met me there that day. Not only did He remind me of all He'd done in my life up to that point but He also clarified the way I was to spend the rest of my life. I sensed His Spirit confirm that I was made to impact how the church develops leaders.

This may sound simplistic, but for me it was life changing. I felt called to reshape what had become the normative method of leadership development. I asked myself, *What if a culture could be created within the church itself that not only identified and equipped leaders but discipled them in a way that allowed them to multiply themselves?*

Patterned after Dr. Hendricks's work, I knew that leadership development had to be simple and reproducible if we were ever going to create a model that allowed average, ordinary men and women in our churches to develop into leaders. A streamlined model was also essential if current leaders, not just staff pastors, were going to see an exponential movement of more and better leaders in their churches and ministries. I committed that day to give my life to multiplying multipliers, and since that day my heart has been burdened to see a multiplication effect of leaders cultivating new leaders.

I've learned a great deal more about leadership development since that moment in the DTS chapel. God has taken the dream He birthed in my heart that day and given me many marvelous opportunities to build on what I learned through my time on staff at Seacoast Church, starting a church-planting network, then as senior director of Church Planter Development at the North American Mission Board, and training numerous churches in leadership development through my work at Auxano. The principles of leaders developing leaders are etched in my heart as I've attempted to create tools to train and model others using the "multiplication effect" process. These principles are at the heart of this book.

Before we begin, however, I want to give you a proper expectation for what this book can and cannot accomplish. The ideas and concepts presented will be short-lived if they are not matched by application. The book isn't designed to simply develop a unique theory of leadership development. Rather, it's meant to give you tools that you can use as you seek to develop leaders in the places of influence in which God has positioned you. You will get the most out of it if you take the time to work through the exercises provided. If you do, you will design an intentional leadership development strategy.

I was on a flight recently to Tampa, Florida, when I struck up a conversation with the gentleman seated next to me. I was fascinated when he told me that his job was to train heart surgeons. One of his coworkers had invented a device and procedure that was revolutionizing heart surgery. Thinking I could learn a thing or two about development from this guy, I asked him to describe the way he trained surgeons to do this complex work. The initial method of all heart surgery was an invasive process that required cracking open the rib cage and working for hours. This was true even for installing a new valve. Now surgeons were able to utilize this new device to make a small incision under the left arm and use a small surgical tool to clip the valve and replace it with a new one. The previous model required four to five hours of surgery and a lengthy period of recovery, but with the new device surgery only took sixteen minutes and recovery was much faster.

Despite these new techniques, he explained, the training for heart surgeons amounted to far more than textbooks and manuals explaining the new device. First, future surgeons had to practice on a model heart using the new procedure. Then they transitioned to practicing on lab animals like sheep or hogs. After the surgery on these experimental animals, future surgeons would take the heart out, observe how they did, and receive feedback. The training process is slow and costly, requiring many hours of training and over sixty thousand dollars to train each physician.

The same is true for developing leaders for the church. It is delicate work, requiring time, intentionality, and intense effort to help new leaders grasp the competencies they need to make kingdom impact. But the cost and time spent developing these leaders is worth it. We'll never be able to mass-produce leaders. If we slow down and build an intentional and reproducible process, then we could see God raise up as many leaders as there is need—leaders with such maturity, proficiency, wisdom, and conviction that they will reshape the landscape of the church in our day. I pray God will use this book to encourage you and help you build and execute an intentional leadership development strategy that will expand His work in your community and beyond.

Part 1

Gifts

Cultivate the God-Given
Gifts in Others

1

Answering the "Why" Question

What's the strategy for developing leaders in your church?

Every leader should be able to answer this question in thirty seconds or less. As I travel, teach, and train around North America, I find that most church leaders struggle to answer this question. In fact, when I ask church leaders this question I generally get one of two responses. Some are honest and say that they don't have one, while others claim their process for developing leaders is organic—which you and I both know means they don't have one. This book is all about helping you, as a leader, answer this question with clarity and conviction. I want to help you build an intentional leadership development strategy that fits your people and your context.

Long before we get to questions of "what" and "how," we must begin with the question of "why." Why do you want to develop leaders in the first place? I know that may sound like a ridiculous question, but your answer to this question may reveal why you're not getting the results you want in the area of leadership development.

In early 1997, my wife, Cindy, and I planted a church in Myrtle Beach, South Carolina. It was an amazing experience right from the beginning. Our little core group of twelve quickly grew to fifty, then seventy, and by the end of the year we had more than two hundred people attending weekend services. But the exciting part was seeing people who had never or rarely been to church surrendering their lives to Christ. In fact, in October of that year we baptized more than sixty people. We loved the adventure of getting into the messiness of people's lives and seeing Christ bring transformation, but it also led to a big problem.

We had a great number of new believers but not enough mature believers to disciple them. To be honest, if someone had asked me at that point why I wanted to develop leaders, I would have laughed at them and simply told them because we didn't have enough! I had never considered there might be a better answer to that question.

Most leaders would probably answer that question the way I did. When they look at the needs of their church, they see a shortage of leaders, which is hindering their mission and overloading their staff. This is probably the most common reason churches attempt to create a plan for leadership development. The current leaders can't get everything done, their span of care is unhealthy, and the quality of the various ministries is suffering. In brief, there is a leadership shortage, and leadership development is the means of addressing this massive problem.

But there's a problem with this answer. When we are driven by the pain of our problem, we are prone to create short-term strategies that get a new batch of leaders in our pipeline quickly. Churches with this mentality find themselves in a start-stop cycle. They focus on leadership development for a season, have inconsequential results, then go back to neglecting it again. Later the pain resurfaces, so the church resuscitates their leadership development efforts once again.

Many churches approach leadership development as a necessary evil to address the symptoms caused by a lack of leaders. Leadership development is not a deep conviction for them. The results are predictable. Anytime you focus on something for a short season and without great intentionality, failure is sure to result. Sure, you might get a leader here or there, but you'll never consistently and effectively produce the quality and quantity of leaders you are looking for.

But there's another way to answer the "why" question. *The greater reason for developing leaders is to cultivate the God-given leadership gifts in others.* Unfortunately, it's rare to hear this type of response. When we're driven by others' potential rather than our pain, leadership development takes on a whole different feel. It is then that our efforts at leadership development become a natural way of thinking. It becomes a part of our regular routine. We don't start with the position that needs to be filled; we start with the person that can be developed. When helping other people maximize their God-given potential is our foundational motive, we are far more likely to succeed over the long haul.

Those operating with this motive are constantly asking others questions such as: What is your passion? What are your strengths? What do you feel God is calling you to do? We instinctively look for opportunities to develop these individuals. We're eager to spend time with them. We celebrate the small baby steps of their growth. Over time we proudly hand off responsibility and authority. And the big win is not filling a leadership position; it's seeing someone maximize the potential of his or her leadership giftedness. With this as the goal, leadership development becomes a natural and consistent part of what we do rather than a necessary evil.

This is what Paul did with Timothy. He didn't develop him to fill a position. He poured his life into Timothy because he loved him, saw him as a son, and had a passion for drawing out the God-given gifts he saw in Timothy. This is why he challenged him: "I remind you to fan into flame the gift of God, which is in you through the laying on of my hands" (2 Timothy 1:6).

What's your "why"? If the pain of the shortage of leaders has driven you, then it's likely you've just been looking at people as a means to the mission rather than seeing them as God-given gifts who need to be developed for kingdom purposes. It's easy for leaders to get focused on their own mission and forget that a big part of leadership is developing other people to fulfill their kingdom mission.

There's an easy way to evaluate your motives in leadership

development. Would you still make it a high priority to develop leaders if all the leadership positions in your church were filled? If the answer is no, then you need to reevaluate why you are developing leaders. But if you said yes, then you are well on your way to building a leadership development strategy that brings out God's best in people.

2

Imagine a Moment

After experiencing rapid growth in the first three years of our church plant, I found myself saying over and over that there was a leadership problem in the church. I wasn't talking about just our church but about the church as a whole. But I no longer believe that statement is true.

There's not a leadership problem in the church, there's a leadership development problem in the church. The leaders are there. Churches are filled with godly men and women who are entrepreneurs, managers, supervisors, coaches, company presidents, moms, all of whom are leading day in and day out. There are believers who sit in our seats every week who are leading in their various contexts. We just need to identify them and help develop them.

Facing this great deficiency of leaders, I asked myself the WWJD question. What would John Maxwell do? I'm kidding. I asked myself what Jesus did to equip leaders for this unstoppable movement. I turned to the Gospels for several months—searching out the answer and underlining every text where I saw Jesus engaged in development. This journey through the Gospels changed my view of leadership development forever. I discovered that Jesus was a master of leadership development who saw something in people and then patiently walked with them to transform their spirit and their skills.

If anyone had excuses for not developing leaders, it was Jesus. Think about it. He was the perfect Son of God, sent to live a perfect life, die a substitutionary death, and defeat Satan, sin, and death through His victorious resurrection. This was work that only He could do, and He knew that He could do it faithfully and fully.

Everywhere He went huge crowds followed, made up of people with all sorts of maladies. His work to declare and demonstrate the love and power of God was massive in scope. And, it's not like there were a ton of people signing up to be on Jesus' leadership team—at least not at the outset, and certainly not once they understood the implications of what it would take to follow Jesus. He had no resources to speak of, lacking even a place to lay His head at night. He could have made excuses for not developing leaders, but He didn't. So what were the marks of Jesus' work in leadership development?

A Defined Culture

As I read through the Gospels, one of the things that struck me was the strategic way Jesus selected His disciples. Luke recorded it this way: "One of those days Jesus went out to a mountainside to pray, and spent the night praying to God. When morning came, he called his disciples to him and chose twelve of them, whom he also designated apostles" (Luke 6:12–13).

Did you see it? "He chose twelve." When Jesus came down from the mountain after a night of prayer, He called His disciples to Himself. How many? We don't know, but we do know it was more than twelve. Can you picture this? Jesus comes down off the mountain, looks into the crowd, and one by one says, "Peter, you come follow Me. Andrew, come follow Me. John, come follow Me." He did this until He had His twelve disciples selected and then basically told everyone else, "Thanks for coming, but you can go home now."

Here we see that very early in Jesus' public ministry He called out and invited twelve men to be His apostles. These men were given a leadership role that was massive in scope—they would be the foundation on which the church was built, and they would be used to declare and demonstrate the good news alongside the Son of God. But why did Jesus take this approach of selecting a small team of leaders?

The parallel passage in Mark tells us: "He appointed twelve that they might *be with Him* and that He might *send them out* to preach and to have authority to drive out demons" (3:14–15, emphasis mine). Jesus knew His time on earth was limited, so He intentionally spent the next three years of His life with these leaders growing their faith, character, leadership, and ability to produce more disciples. Jesus was starting off His ministry building a culture of leadership development.

An Intentional Structure

The process did not end with the call of this small team of apostles. Notice in the flow of the next few passages how Jesus was weaving together a structure to advance the gospel. Historians tell us that there were about 240 villages scattered across the region of Galilee. Jesus traveled alone throughout these villages healing the sick and proclaiming the good news (Luke 4). Shortly thereafter, Jesus did another tour through Galilee with His disciples tagging along to watch and learn (Luke 5–8). These first two trips represent a ratio of 1 to 240. That's one evangelist taking the gospel to 240 villages. That's quite a task. Next, we see a shift in the structure. Jesus now sent these twelve back through the villages with the same task—yet this time Jesus did not go with them (Luke 9:1–6).

It's likely that these twelve apostles divided up the villages and executed the strategy Jesus gave them. Now we see six teams taking on the evangelization of Galilee. So instead of a 1 to 240 ratio there is a 1 to 40 ratio. One team for every forty villages.

Now fast-forward a few months to the event recorded in Luke 10, when Jesus commissioned more leaders—this time seventy-two of them—to continue the work of the apostles. He strategically sent them in pairs ahead of Him into the villages to preach and heal (Luke 10:1–12). Wow, now instead of a 1 to 240 ratio or a 1 to 40 ratio, there is a 1 to 6 ratio. This multiplication of leaders was helping advance the gospel throughout Galilee.

But, hold on, it doesn't end there. What is fascinating is the instruction Jesus gave the seventy-two before He sent them out. "The Lord appointed seventy-two others and sent them . . . to every town and place where he was about to go. He told them, 'The harvest is plentiful, but the workers are few. Ask the Lord of the harvest, therefore, to send out workers into his harvest field'" (Luke 10:1–2).

The word Jesus used for "send out" means "to draw out" or "to pluck out." Sometimes the word is used to speak of forcefully tearing something out. Jesus was telling the seventy-two, "As you go into the villages, ask God to raise up more leaders—more people who will advance the gospel." The implication was that the gospel had spread throughout Galilee and some had received that gospel. Now as this new batch of disciples carried out the mission part of their role, they called out others to take that bold step of leading in ways that would advance the gospel.

Jesus was not haphazard in the way He chose to use His first followers. He had a plan—a plan to consistently multiply and expand leaders who would advance the mission.

A Systematic Approach

Jesus was systematic in His selection and development of His first leaders. He did not merely sound the alarm and say, "Hey, I need a few leaders. Who's in?" He was intentional to pursue relationships with these men and call them out to something great.

Jesus first met four of His disciples at His baptism in the wilderness just outside Jerusalem. When they inquired about who He is,

He said, "Come and see." This was an invitation to get to know Him better. From there, Jesus headed north and stopped in Judea along the way. This would have been a thirty-six-mile walk where these men would have peppered Him with questions.

Then Jesus returned to Galilee where He interacted with these men even more. After getting to know them, Jesus called these men to follow Him as His disciples and then later as His apostles. He didn't just randomly and spontaneously choose these men and invest in them—He had spent time getting to know them and letting them get to know Him. He walked with them, taught them, modeled evangelism with them, prayed for them, and invited them to lead alongside Him. When we provide a systematic way for potential leaders to join us on our team, it gives us time to get to know them so we can better understand how God wants to use them in His mission.

Purposeful Content

Jesus is often referred to as a master teacher because of the impact He had and the variety of techniques He used. Continually throughout His ministry, insiders and onlookers were amazed at His teaching (Mark 1:22; Luke 4:32). They were certainly amazed at the content of His teaching, as He announced the availability of the kingdom of God (Mark 1:15). The reality that all Israel had longed to experience was now present in the person of Jesus Christ. They were also stunned at His authority. He did not teach like the other rabbis of His day; He taught with a zeal and conviction as the true Son of God.

Jesus' teaching did not take place in a classroom. Most of His training was on the job. He told stories and used the concrete realities of His day to communicate deep spiritual truth. Everywhere He went He was teaching, and those who heard His words were instructed in the core realities of the kingdom of God.

A Multiplying People

Finally, Jesus was not content with the first generation of followers. Following His victorious resurrection, Jesus called His disciples together and gave them a mission: "Therefore go and make disciples of all nations" (Matthew 28:19). He challenged them to multiply themselves in the lives of others—promising to go with them as they were faithful to obey this commission.

The spread of the church in the first century is evidence that these disciples were faithful to multiply for the sake of this mission. They were leaders who were capable of making other leaders who, in turn, could make other leaders as well (2 Timothy 2:2). The apostles and early followers of Jesus would give their lives to continue the process of developing leaders through ongoing training. They were not content to rest on their past successes but continued to train leaders to excel in Jesus' character and in their respective leadership roles.

There you have it—the framework we will use to help you create a multiplication effect in your church: culture, structure, systems, content, and people.

Of course, the Bible is not designed to give us every facet of Jesus' leadership development model. Yet we can apply these five main categories to our modern challenges regarding leadership development. The remainder of this book will seek to do just that. We will look at five key skills around each of these categories—culture, structure, systems, content, and people—that are required to build an effective leadership development process in your local church. In each section we will begin by dissecting the problem and then provide three or four clear action steps you can take to foster leadership development among the people God has given you.

3

Discipleship or Leadership
Development (or Both)

There is much more we could say about Jesus' work in leadership development, yet the principles in chapter 2 are enough to establish the main contours of all that follows. We will return to these themes time and again as we begin to outline a paradigm for leadership development in our churches. But before we begin to build this framework, you might find yourself asking the question, "But can we really say that Jesus was developing leaders? Wasn't He making disciples?" I'm convinced that these two—leadership development and disciple making—go hand in hand.

Jesus was a master disciple-maker. This point is without debate. As we saw in the last chapter, there's much we can learn from Jesus' model of discipleship. But there is often pushback when we segue into a discussion of leadership development. The assumption is that discipleship is a biblical notion whereas leadership development is merely a fad of secular business principles.

I sensed a resistance when taking a church through the Leadership Pipeline process. During a break I mentioned to the pastor that I was feeling some tension. He described his staff as biblically astute and skeptical of leadership development—feeling it was too much of a corporate concept not derived clearly from the pages of Scripture. I run into that often. It's an unfortunate either-or that I find unnecessary. In this chapter I will describe the subtle differences between leadership development and discipleship, but also explain that leadership development is simply the discipling of leaders.

The reality is that it's impossible to separate these two. This hit me when I looked back over my life and realized that I had experienced three conversions in my life. I know this might sound like heresy, but let me explain.

Lost to Found

My first conversion took place when I was only nine years old. I stood in the second row of Handley Baptist Church gripping the pew in front of me. The pastor of our little country church had just given a very clear presentation of the gospel, and God grabbed my heart. Before I knew it, I had walked down the aisle, and Pastor Randy Kessler led me into a life-changing relationship with Jesus Christ. I confessed my sins and surrendered my life fully to God. *On that Sunday morning, I experienced my first conversion as I moved from lost to found.*

Doer to Leader

Over the years I grew in my faith and eventually surrendered to God's call on my life to pursue vocational ministry. I was doing all I could to serve the church, but people were constantly telling me that I was not a leader. I may not have been a leader at that time, but that all changed in 1986 when I moved to Dallas, Texas, to attend Dallas Theological Seminary. There I met a pastor who evidently saw potential in me and began to spend time with me. He asked me to meet with him for an hour at his office every Tuesday. There wasn't a clear agenda to these meetings—we'd just sit and talk about leadership and life. He gave me books, articles, and audio lessons and asked me to review them and come to our meetings with questions. This pastor's mentoring was unlike anything I had experienced. He wasn't just teaching me to live like Jesus, he was teaching me to lead like Jesus.

Over time I noticed that my questions were met with answers like this: "That's a good question. What do you think?" Then a few months later he turned it up a notch. When I'd ask a question, he would reply, "You're the expert. What do you think?" What? Me, the expert? No way. But he truly began to treat me as if he respected my thinking, which transformed the way I saw myself. Not only did his life have an indelible impact on mine but he modeled the power of mentoring in a way that forever shaped the way I would develop leaders. For the first time in my life I truly began to lead. *I underwent my second conversion during this time, as I moved from doer to leader.*

Leader to Leader Developer

But the story wasn't over. There was a third conversion coming four years later. I was fresh out of seminary and taking on my first full-time ministry position as an associate pastor in a growing church in the Southeast. I was young, enthusiastic, and thought I could do it all. It didn't take long for me to become overcommitted and overwhelmed by the tremendous responsibility of leading in the church. I had my hands in everything, including weekend worship, midweek teaching, and leading the small-group ministry, Sunday school ministry, youth ministry, and the summer children's program. I was leading teams of people in nearly every area of the church. I had a slight case of Superman complex.

Everything went well for the first few months. But after a year I looked at my wife, Cindy, and said, "Honey, this church is going to fire me." She darted back, "What? They're not going to fire you, they love you." I explained that I was juggling all sorts of leadership responsibilities and I knew I was going to drop something. I simply couldn't keep up. Leading was crushing me. I explained there was simply too much to do and not enough me to go around. I couldn't keep going at this pace, especially at the rate the church was growing. My inability to develop others had painted me into a corner, and I was headed for trouble.

That night I couldn't sleep, so I sat in the hallway and wrote out the names of everyone who reported to me in the church. I was shocked when I saw a total of eighty-eight names on the list. God showed me two things that night: first, I had to make leadership development a priority, and second, I had to develop a strategy that was worth prioritizing.

That night I decided it was time to stop leading everything myself and start developing others to lead. I recruited seven leaders to oversee the key ministry areas and committed that if they would lead that area of ministry, I would do all I could to support, encourage, and develop them. And from that point on I started pouring into those leaders so they could pour into their teams. For the first time in my life I truly started doing leadership development, and it saved my life and my ministry. *My third conversion moved me from leader to leader developer.*

What About You?

One of the greatest obstacles to developing leaders in the church is the fact that too many believers have not experienced this second or third conversion. This keeps them operating as doers rather than developers in the church. Many leaders are missing out on the joy of discipling leaders.

But we all intuitively know that this is killing us. We may get many good things done. We might help people. We might even run a wide array of effective programs. But each of us is only one person. There's simply no way one person can do everything.

And the reality is, we are most effective at doing only the things we can do. If we try to do too much more, then the ministry will quickly exceed our capacity. If we are going to have any hope of fulfilling the Great Commission, then we must develop leaders.

This is why I believe it's time for a revolution—a change in the way we develop leaders. For too long now we have looked to classroom lectures to equip the leaders needed to carry out the mission. While this methodology has its place, it has failed us in producing the level of transformation and multiplication that we see in the lives of the twelve Jesus discipled.

As I look back over what God did in my life, it's obvious that I have been and always will be a disciple. But what He did in my life up to the point of age twenty-eight took on a little different dynamic after age twenty-eight. I was fully surrendered and doing my best to live like Jesus at that time. As my pastor in Dallas met with me, discipleship began to take on a different shape. Four shifts took place in my life that reveal the subtle difference between discipleship and leadership development, but these two concepts were united in my life. I was being discipled as a leader.

SHIFT #1: FROM LEADING MYSELF TO LEADING OTHERS

Until the time I was twenty-eight, my life was primarily focused on leading myself. Through my church and friends who were Christ followers, I learned how to walk with God daily, how to study the Bible, and how to grow myself in the faith. But when my pastor in Dallas began to meet with me, he was teaching me how to lead others. He taught me how to cast a vision others would follow, how to think strategically, and how to lead a team. For the first time in my life I was learning to lead others.

SHIFT #2: FROM INTIMACY WITH CHRIST TO INFLUENCE FOR CHRIST

By the time I was twenty-eight, God had developed in me a deep passion for my relationship with Him. I was hungry to know Him more and had developed disciplines that enabled me to walk in the Spirit. But through my newfound mentoring relationship, I was discovering the subtleties of how to influence others. It was no longer just that I wanted to follow Jesus; I wanted to influence others to follow Jesus.

SHIFT #3: FROM LIVING LIKE JESUS TO LEADING LIKE JESUS

I was by no means perfect at this point, but I knew the basics of living like Jesus. I was learning the truth that whoever claims to follow Jesus must also live like He did (1 John 2:6). My life was increasingly marked by a desire to pursue holiness. But now this pursuit of holiness was connected with my influence of others. I wanted to help others know and love Jesus.

I began to study the Gospels with a new perspective. I had always looked at the life of Jesus, seeking to live as He lived. But suddenly I saw the influence and impact Jesus had on the leaders around Him. I saw how He passionately shared His mission and people would give up everything to follow Him. That's when it hit me: if I want my life to have a fuller impact, I must learn to lead like Jesus.

SHIFT #4: FROM CHARACTER TO COMPETENCIES

Up to this point the focus of my spiritual growth was primarily on character. God had used my church and friends to work to shape in me the fruit of the Spirit: love, joy, peace, patience, kindness, gentleness, goodness, faithfulness, and self-control (Galatians 5:22–23). But now, as He continued to grow my character, there was a newfound focus on developing leadership competencies I had never known: team building, problem solving, managing time, resolving conflict, communication, and execution. These competencies would be necessary for me to build and lead teams of people to accomplish kingdom work.

Connecting Discipleship and Leadership Development

My heart is burdened because I see that we have intentional discipleship taking place in churches with programs such as Navigators 2:7, Rooted, Starting Point, Multiply, and others. But rarely is there an intentional pathway for discipling leaders.

Leadership development should be an extension of a church's discipleship strategy because leadership development is about discipling leaders. Seen in this light, discipleship and leadership development fuel each other. As you invest in one, the other is a natural by-product. As you will see throughout this book, there are many places where the principles we discuss will be applicable to your work in discipleship as well. However, the void of tools that are particularly targeted to address the leadership development process is the unique target of *The Multiplication Effect*.

This focus is intentional. While discipleship and leadership development have much in common, it's critical that we have a laser-like focus. If we want to develop leaders that reproduce themselves, we must have that goal at the forefront of our minds to create an intentional plan that fosters that goal. You'd never build a factory and say, "I'm not really sure what we want to make, but we sure do have a nice building, great machines, and a spectacular staff. Just throw some raw materials in there and surely something good will result." No. As a manufacturer you'd have specific ends in mind and design everything else you do to produce the final product you're after.

I once heard a statement that has always stuck with me:

If you always do what you've always done, you'll always get what you've always gotten.

Don't skim over this. Read it one more time. This statement is true in many areas of life and ministry. It is certainly true of leadership development.

It seems everyone is struggling with the same question: How do you develop leaders? We want good leaders, qualified leaders, leaders who are committed, leaders who get it, leaders who possess the DNA of our church, and leaders who produce results and eventually multiply themselves. We try everything to develop leaders—hold classes, create seminars, and go to conferences. But do these work? These efforts aren't bad in and of themselves, but they often fail to produce the number and quality of leaders that we need. Something must change.

That's the goal of this book. I want to change the conversation regarding leadership development. I long for others to experience the same conversion I did and move to being a developer of leaders. I want us to consider our method of developing leaders and see if we can find a better way. Ultimately, I want to be a part of seeing men, women, and children come to faith in Jesus Christ. I want to play my part in the work of making disciples and developing leaders through the church until the day when Jesus returns. The fact that you've picked up this book means that I don't have to convince you of this need. What I hope to do is leverage our shared awareness of the need to produce a renewed passion and plan for the work to which we've given our lives.

Part 2
Culture

Build a Culture of Leadership
Development That Generates an Abundant
Harvest of Reproducing Leaders

4

A Do-It-Yourself
Leadership Culture

One of the greatest lessons I've learned about leadership culture came when I was a twenty-one-year-old coach of the Handley Yankees Little League team. My team was made up of the typical assortment of young, energetic athletes with modest ability—except for Andy. He was a naturally gifted athlete. His fielding and hitting were head and shoulders above his peers.

Near the end of the season, Andy led us into a game against our rivals, the Pratt Reds. The game was tight heading into the sixth and final inning. We were leading by only one run, and Andy was growing more and more intense with every pitch he threw. We only needed one more out as Andy toed the rubber to deliver the game-winning pitch. But this time the batter got the best of him and drilled a rocket shot to deep center. This just happened to be where one of our slower players was positioned. There was no home run fence in this league, so the ball seemed to roll on forever.

Andy assessed the situation and decided to take matters into his own hands. He ran into center field, past the player who was supposed to be retrieving the ball. When he gathered the ball, he turned to run back toward the infield himself rather than throwing it back to any teammates. As the batter rounded second, Andy was sprinting for home plate rather than throwing it to the cut-off or even to the third baseman. Yet, because of Andy's immense skill, he was able to outrun the batter and tag him out just as he slid into home. As expected, the crowd went crazy. The Yankees had won the game and Andy was a hero.

Despite Andy's amazing play, there was a clear problem—he ignored his fellow teammates, neglected their giftedness, and inadvertently communicated that they weren't even needed on the team.

Pastors and ministry leaders are prone to the same mistake. God raises up exceptionally gifted leaders to care for His church, and, like Andy, they often try to do everything alone. The motives vary. Some are afraid to trust their teammates. Others do it all themselves to prove their value. And some are simply addicted to being the hero. As a result, everything rises and falls on a single leader, and leadership development is nonexistent.

In 2009, Leadership Network conducted a survey with five thousand people. They repeated it in 2019 with the same results. They asked, "Would you like to know when we release resources on a certain topic?" They gave them twenty-five options to choose from. Care to guess what the number one answer was?

Leadership development. The results of this survey show that churches are struggling with leadership development. This is not surprising. Despite the awareness of the need for leadership development, our do-it-yourself culture of church leadership often fails to make any significant traction in identifying a solution.

The Problem of Growth

The church must identify a solution. Imagine a church that begins with one hundred people and a strong leadership base. This would be a church planter's dream! Then imagine they grow to two hundred, then four hundred, and finally five hundred people in the span of just a few years. Yet what if this church maintains the same leadership base they had when they were a church of one hundred? The results would be disastrous over time. They would no longer have a leadership base capable of caring for those whom God sends. The church becomes an inverted pyramid, with a narrow base supporting a large number of people at the top. If any church continues to grow up and does not, at the same time, grow out, then it will eventually collapse under its own weight.

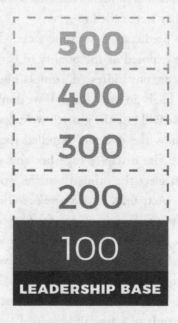

The long-term health and spiritual vitality of any church is dependent on leadership development. Far too often we spend our time and energy focusing on upward growth while ignoring our leadership base. Desiring upward growth is not wrong, but what would happen if we focused on growing up and out at the same time?

In Acts 6 we have a perfect case study of what can happen when the church grows up and not out. Luke wrote, "In those days when the number of disciples was increasing, the Hellenistic Jews among them complained against the Hebraic Jews because their widows were being overlooked in the daily distribution of food" (Acts 6:1).

The first church experienced phenomenal growth. The growth revealed leadership deficiencies in the church. While the growth went up, the quality of ministry went down. And when the quality went down, the complaining went up. The complaints were well-founded—widows were being neglected. It's not that these were petty gripes. They were complaints that hindered the effectiveness of the church to minister to those they were called to serve.

This pattern is predictable. Anytime a church grows, leadership deficiencies will be exposed as the quality of care goes down. Over time, if these issues are not addressed, complaining will invariably go up and growth will likely go back down. If we don't address leadership deficiencies, then we will lose the growth we've gained.

Now look at how the disciples handled the situation: "So the Twelve gathered all the disciples together and said, 'It would not be right for us to neglect the ministry of the word of God in order to wait on tables'" (Acts 6:2). *Growth will require you to make hard choices about what you will and will not do.* They could have adopted a far easier solution than what they chose. There were twelve apostles and twelve months in the year, so they could have simply asked each apostle to take a month and care for the widows. Need met!

Such a decision would be an Andy-like move. It would have kept leadership in the hands of a few and avoided the task of leadership development. They understood that they had certain responsibilities, and, should they tackle the widows' needs themselves, they would most certainly get distracted and neglect their primary responsibilities. Today's leaders face the same temptation. When they decide to be the solution rather than work to create a solution that requires more leaders, growth is stunted.

The apostles decided to collaborate to find a solution rather than being the solution themselves. After making it clear that they would not take on the additional responsibility, the apostles said, "Brothers and sisters, choose seven men from among you who are known to be full of the Spirit and wisdom. We will turn this responsibility over to them" (Acts 6:3). They appointed new leaders to take on the responsibilities.

Growth provides opportunity for more people to develop and deploy their gifts. Many of those appointed in this passage were relative no-names. They were leaders who met a real need in the church. They were servants marked by integrity and character. Some, like Philip, went on to travel, preach, and evangelize. Others died in obscurity. But they met a real need in the church, addressed an area of complaint, and allowed the church to continue to grow. Luke wrote: "So the word of God spread. The number of disciples in Jerusalem increased rapidly" (Acts 6:7).

The apostles understood that their role in leadership and developing leaders was so they could give "attention to prayer and the ministry of the word" (Acts 6:4). *Growth requires that leaders refine what they are called to, gifted for, and focused on.* As this happens, the leadership base grows to support the upward growth God is sending.

If you find yourself too busy doing things you are not gifted to do, then you may be hindering the effectivness of the church by failing to develop leaders. There are people out there who can already do many things better than you. They have been sent by God to address your deficiencies and meet the needs of the body of Christ. The bottom line is, if you care for the spiritual health, vitality, and growth of your church, then you will identify, recruit, and disciple leaders.

Churches are struggling with this issue of leadership development. For leadership development to work—and I mean really work—it cannot be another task to add to an already bloated to-do list. Rather, *discipling leaders must become a defining mark of your church's culture.* It's impossible to overemphasize this statement, so we need to spend some time unpacking exactly what we mean. In this section I will give you a tool to evaluate your leadership development culture and then offer some practical steps to build a culture of leadership development that generates an abundant harvest of reproducing leaders.

5

Missing a Mark We've Never Defined

As I travel, I often ask pastors to describe the leadership development strategy of their churches. One pastor looked at me with great confidence and said they called their model the "Yoyo strategy." I'd never heard this one, so I asked him for more detail. His wry smile indicated that the joke was on me. The church's model was "You're On Your Own." His wit unknowingly expressed the normative culture of leadership development in most churches. If we're going to have any hope at developing leaders, then we must do better.

Forced to Define Leadership Development

When I was pastoring Carolina Forest Community Church, I was feeling the pressure of not having a leadership development strategy. The good news was, we were in a season of growth; the bad news was that I was not prepared for how to develop leaders to keep up with the growth. It seemed we were baptizing a lot of new believers but didn't have a proportionate number of mature leaders to help with the disciple-making process.

As I wrestled with the challenge, the question of what leadership development is came to mind. I turned to the internet to search "definition of leadership development." This was pre-Google, so I found nothing. But I am glad I didn't find anything, because it forced me to write my own definition. I took out a pen and paper and scratched out this definition:

> Leadership development is an intentional process in which one interacts with an experienced leader producing transformation in the character and competencies that increase their ability to influence people, outcomes, and culture.

I discovered once I defined leadership development and understood the components of it I could now evaluate our leadership development efforts against this specific definition. Let's tease out the various facets of this definition:

- **Intentional process:** Your church has a defined and specific approach to the way you develop new and existing leaders.
- **Interacts with:** There is a deeply rooted belief that leadership development is best done in the context of relationships. It's nearly impossible to help someone change their leadership behaviors unless you are close enough to observe and interact with those you're training.
- **An experienced leader:** Proven leaders are guiding the process and investing in others.
- **Character and competencies:** You strive for a balance between equipping their being and doing, between developing the spirit and skill of the potential leader.
- **Increase effectiveness:** The goal is growth, which will be the result of transformation brought over an extended period of time.
- **Influencing people, outcomes, and culture:** Our development efforts must help leaders be more effective at influencing the attitudes, thoughts, and behavior patterns of people. But it goes beyond that; a leader is also responsible for the corporate culture

of his or her organization or team. Every leader must learn how to influence the corporate personality and values of the organization. And finally, leaders are responsible for results, so every leader must increase their ability to influence the results of their organization.

You won't do a good job with leadership development until you understand what it is. Now try your hand at it. How would you define leadership development? Write out your definition in a journal.

Frustrated with Leadership Development Outcomes

Lifeway research in 2012 revealed 92 percent of pastors think training and development are critical to the health and growth of the church. But only 25 percent say they have a plan to develop leaders.[1] Pastors are not confident that the lay leaders they have put in place have the competencies to really do the job well. Often our leadership development efforts are simply geared toward helping leaders comply with the policies and procedures of the ministry. We just want them to fill the position and stay between the lines. But training people toward compliance does not create an empowered leader who is really leading and making a lasting impact.

Once you create a definition of leadership development for your church and begin to practice it in the way you have defined, then you will begin to see different outcomes for your efforts. Leadership development should result in a noticeable change in a leader's beliefs and behaviors. If a leader's beliefs and behaviors have not changed, then we've not done leadership development. Are your development efforts focused on compliance or wisdom? Are you teaching people rules or principles? Do you want them to turn a widget according to standard, or do you want them to think for themselves and innovate? Your training is shaping their thinking. Leadership development loses its potency when I am only focused on getting people to do what I want them to do rather than helping them maximize their abilities and understand themselves.

In church we usually equip people to turn our ministry widgets. As long as things go smoothly, we are good. We just want them to do the job. But that's really not leadership; that is functional administration. What outcomes are you expecting from the leadership development efforts of your church?

Assessment

There's a lot that goes into building a culture of discipling leaders. This book is meant to address many of those factors. But before we consider action steps, it's important that you pause to consider the strengths and weaknesses of your church in terms of leadership development. I developed a simple assessment that I give to churches to help them discover the current reality of their leadership development culture. Give it a try and see how you would rate your church. If you are reading this book with others, ask them to do the assessment as well and then get together and discuss your observations using the questions at the end of the chapter.

Mark each statement using the following system:

1. Not true of us
2. Rarely true of us
3. True of us
4. Very true of us
5. We are a model for others to follow

- The senior leaders are supportive and involved in developing leaders themselves.
- Leaders at every level of our church/organization are expected to be involved in developing/discipling new leaders.

- We have a specific leadership development strategy we are using consistently in our church/organization.
- We cast vision for leadership development on a regular basis.
- We have developed a language around our leadership development efforts that has become engrained in our culture.
- We have a very clear onboarding process for leaders at every level of our church/organization.
- We are providing accountability by measuring the results of our leadership development efforts.
- We celebrate the successes of our leadership development efforts on a consistent basis.
- We have someone who is consistently championing the cause of leadership development.
- We have a mentality that leadership development is more of a marathon than a sprint.

Now, total up your score and use the following categories to assess your results.

STRONG LEADERSHIP DEVELOPMENT CULTURE (SCORE OF 45–50)

You already have a very strong leadership development culture. You need to focus on fine-tuning the details and consider doing some outside-the-box thinking for the future of leadership development at your church. You also need to consider how you can help other churches improve their leadership development processes.

HIGH POTENTIAL FOR A LEADERSHIP DEVELOPMENT CULTURE (SCORE OF 39–44)

Your church is close to having a leadership development culture. You're doing a good job in some areas of leadership development but probably have some weak spots that are keeping it from truly being engrained in your culture. It is likely that some people in your church have bought in, while others still do not see leadership development as a part of their job. You need to choose the one or two areas that are lagging behind and find ways to maximize your efforts there.

GOOD POTENTIAL FOR A LEADERSHIP DEVELOPMENT CULTURE (SCORE OF 33–38)

Don't be discouraged, because you have some strengths you can build on. While it may be important to you, others in the church don't see leadership development as a priority. Make sure everyone in the church understands what is going well in the area of leadership development, and then cast a vision for taking it to a new level. The fact that you are doing some things well will help your current leaders easily get excited about improving leadership development in your culture. Choose one or two areas you feel are most important and gather a team of people who can help you make the necessary changes.

NEED IMPROVEMENT TO REACH A LEADERSHIP DEVELOPMENT CULTURE (SCORE OF 27–32)

While your church may be growing and doing good things, it may be in danger of losing effectiveness in the future unless you raise your leadership development efforts. It will be important that senior leadership begin to emphasize leadership development as a priority. Leadership development has not been a part of your culture, and it is going to take some hard work and patience to begin to build it into your culture.

SERIOUS NEED TO CHANGE YOUR CULTURE (SCORE OF 0–26)

This is a strong indication that your church may be in decline or is built upon a dynamic and charismatic leader. You are facing an uncertain future, and the senior leadership team needs to begin to have some serious talks about the future of the church. You may need to bring someone in from the outside to coach you in the initial steps of building a leadership development foundation in your church. The senior leadership needs to begin to study the importance of leadership development and to make it a priority in their own day-to-day practices.

Discuss your score with other leaders in your church. See if your scores are similar to theirs, and use the following questions to guide the discussion.

- What are the strengths of your church in developing leaders?
- What do you feel is the biggest growth area in the development of leaders for you as a church?
- What is the most important thing your church can do today that will make the biggest difference in building a culture of leadership development for tomorrow?

The remainder of this section will present four essentials for creating a culture of leadership development: you must talk about it, model it, expect it, and fight for it.

6

Talk About Building Culture,
Not About Building Leaders

So far in this section we've noted the main problem with a leadership development culture, written a definition of leadership development, and assessed the current reality of our churches by asking ten questions. Now it's time to get to work building a leadership development culture. And culture is the place we want to begin.

As you talk about your church's leadership development needs and efforts, what do you find yourself talking about? What you talk about will tend to lead you toward the results you're getting. If you're talking about the shortage of leaders and the empty positions that need to be filled, then you're likely to have your existing leaders trying to simply fill spots. If you're talking about your leadership problems, then you're likely to have your existing leaders trying to develop stop-gap solutions. But what if you stopped talking so much about developing leaders and started talking more about creating a leadership development culture that resulted in a multiplication effect?

Then you are more likely to end up with a culture of reproducing leaders. We will never create movement unless we develop a culture in which leadership development is normative. In fact, when I am taking churches through the Leadership Pipeline training, I tell them our end goal is to produce an abundant harvest of reproducing leaders.

Imagine what it would be like to have not just one person developing leaders in your church, but five or ten or twenty people, and over time many of the leaders they developed turned around and began developing new leaders themselves. That's when you know you have a culture of leadership development.

If you want to see a constant stream of leaders emerging in your church, then you must change your language and stop talking about developing leaders and start talking more about building a culture of leadership development. *The reason most churches have a leadership deficiency today is because they never built a culture of leadership development yesterday.* There are no leaders because developing leaders has not been engrained in their culture. And if we don't build a culture of leadership development today, we will have a deficiency of leaders in our pipeline tomorrow.

You see, when you focus merely on building leaders, you often simply develop leaders to fill a spot. Once the spot is filled, you no longer focus on developing leaders. A leader has an empty spot on his team, so he starts to look around to fill the empty position. He thinks, *He's not ready . . . She's not ready . . . Oh . . . He's ready!* He then places that person in the empty position. He relaxes because the spot has been filled and he no longer has to do leadership development.

This behavior isn't leadership *development*—it's leader *placement*. We find ready-made leaders and plug them into ministry spots. It's less about development and more about filling spots to turn a ministry widget. The answer is to talk about building a leadership development culture and not simply filling slots with leaders.

One Developer's Story

When I was working at Westridge Church in Atlanta, I was walking out to my car one day after work when a lady came running up to me almost in tears but with a huge smile on her face. She told me she wanted to thank me for helping with the leadership development efforts at the church. She had gone through the small-group leader training, and now as an experienced leader she was training new small-group leaders herself. During the past year she had raised up five new small-group leaders and was finding so much joy in reproducing herself in this way. As she led her group, she was being used to multiply new leaders. She told me she had never felt more fulfilled in ministry and couldn't believe a church would empower and entrust her with the raising up of new leaders.

This story portrays the end result we are after. *We want a culture that results in an abundant harvest of reproducing leaders.* This is the bull's-eye. It's the goal. We want to foster a culture that functions as a teaching organization, meaning that leaders are focused on teaching potential leaders to lead and equipping them to do the same for others.

It's not a win when you produce a leader. It's a win when the newly produced leader produces a leader. That's how you know you have a leadership development culture. Imagine for a moment you hire Sue to do leadership development for your church. She enthusiastically takes on the role, and you are thrilled as you watch her raise up Joyce, Mary, and Kathy as new leaders. During the year Sue continues to crank out more leaders. But a year later Sue and her husband decide they need to move away to be closer to family. What happens to leadership development in your church? It stops. Why? Because you had a leadership developer but not a leadership development culture.

But if Sue took a different approach and she focused on developing Joyce, who then developed Mary, who then developed Kathy, now you're beginning to see a true culture of leadership development being established in your church. If Sue moves away, you would certainly miss her and her family, but leadership development would continue because she focused on developing developers and not just developing leaders. Take anyone out and the process continues because leadership development is the focus, not an individual.

But to get this type of culture you must *talk about* building a leadership development culture. Every chance you get, talk about it when you are with a team member one-on-one or when you're having a team meeting. There are four ways you can talk about leadership development that will begin to build this kind of culture.

Talk About the Current Reality

Not many churches would say they have a leadership development culture. But most would say that's what they would like. It's important to acknowledge where you're at as a church on this journey. If you're just starting out, that's okay. I heard Peter Senge say one of the leader's first jobs is to define the current reality. Talking to your team about the areas for growth is the first step in making progress. Perhaps the best way to start is to have them take the Organizational Leadership Development Assessment in chapter 5 and talk about it as a team.

Talk About the Vision

Defining reality is the starting point, but now you must show your team where you're headed. Cast a vision showing them what it could look like if you worked together to create a culture of developing leaders. Let them see your enthusiasm. Help them see that while it may be long and hard work, you feel it's a possibility and you're committed to making it happen.

Talk About the Goal

While it's great to have a vision, you also need goals that will serve as milestones along the way. It will be important to define how many leaders you'd like to develop over a set period of time. But it's just as important, if not more important, to clarify how many leader developers you'd like to establish. Chapter 33 contains more instruction on how to do that.

Talk About the Wins

Once you have some goals, you need to bang the drum and celebrate when your team hits those goals. In fact, I'd start beating the drum early, praising progress along the way, inspiring them to keep up the good work. I tell my team all the time we have to praise progress, not perfection. Talk about progress regularly in your team meetings, giving people updates and pointing out the wins along the way. I like to tell my team celebrating wins gives us wind to keep going.

By talking about the current reality, vision, goals, and wins, your team will begin to see this focus on leadership development is not a fad that will go away. Instead it's a culture you're building together.

7

Model Leadership
Development from the Top

If you want to build a culture of leadership development, it's essential that you are modeling leadership development. Imagine a church that is growing at a rate of 15 percent each year with no signs of slowing down. It is seeing people come to faith and is now considering planting a new church on the other side of town. The senior pastor, knowing the necessity of leadership development, calls his staff together and tells them that leadership development must be a priority during the coming year. He casts a compelling vision for the necessity of leadership development and gives the staff a goal of leaders they need to produce by the end of the year. The meeting concludes with each staff member challenged to pursue this new goal.

Nothing about the meeting is wrong. But there are two different ways that this senior pastor can engage in leadership development. In the first, he is simply the guy who holds others responsible for their work in developing leaders. He can cast vision, lead meetings, and push others to hit their marks when it comes to leadership development. Or the senior pastor can invest in the work of leadership development personally. He can take ownership of the role he plays in helping the staff meet their leadership development goals and model for them the behaviors he desires the entire staff to embody.

Which model is more apt to produce a culture of leadership development? The second. In the first model, the senior pastor is a passive observer of the work of leadership development. Though he is invested in the process, his actions demonstrate that he believes the work of leadership development begins with others. His staff is likely to interpret his lack of investment in the process as evidence that while the desire for leadership development is clear, the priority for implementing this culture does not extend to the top.

But, in reality, culture building starts at the top. Senior leaders can cast vision for leadership development relentlessly, but unless they are personally invested in the process of developing leaders, it is unlikely that a true culture will ever form. There is a bullish, uncompromising law that you can't ignore as you consider building a leadership development culture: *the values of the leader become the values of the organization.*

The true values of a church are not those that are posted in the hallway by the water cooler but those the leader lives out day to day. Unfortunately, there's often a big difference between the two. A leader may order the execution of a new leadership development program, set an organization-wide goal for the development of leaders, or even assign a task force to identify solutions to the leadership development problem; however, if he is not involved in developing leaders, then that organization will never cultivate a leadership development culture.

A gap between aspirational values and lived values will hinder the development of a leadership development culture. People are perceptive: if they notice that the key leader isn't living the values he or she is communicating, then they will often lose heart and fail to pursue leadership development with the zeal necessary to create the culture the leader desires.

Don't worry, senior leaders, this doesn't mean that you have to suddenly put aside significant portions of your role to take on this new added responsibility. Rather, you can incorporate leadership development into your daily work. It's not the volume of leaders you produce; it's your voice and visibility in the process. Begin by working to develop at least one other person in your church. If you don't model it yourself, then you simply can't expect it from others.

Rick Duncan's story reveals the truth that leadership development flows down, not up. Rick planted Cuyahoga Valley Church (CVC) near Cleveland, Ohio, in the mid-1980s. A few years ago he passed the torch of senior pastor to a younger leader, Chad, after spending two years equipping him to lead the church. For the first few years after the transition, Rick stayed full-time on staff at the church, led the missions department, and developed the Leadership Pipeline, which they called the CVC Leadership Greenhouse. Rick said,

> One of my biggest regrets as lead pastor is that I did not learn what Mac teaches about the Leadership Pipeline early in my ministry. The big gaps for us at CVC were we did not have strong leaders of leaders, and we did not have a training track to develop leaders of departments.
>
> Put practically, we had 1,100 LifeGroup members in more than 100 LifeGroups being overseen by three staff members. You know what that means, right? Our leaders were pretty much on their own. Our LifeGroup leaders were not being cared for, resourced, or developed. No wonder we had a lot of turnover. No wonder our LifeGroup growth had hit a wall.[1]

Since applying the principles of this book, Rick said,

> We have developed the core competencies for each of the levels of leadership in the life of our church. In a mentoring format, we have raised up and trained more than twenty leaders of leaders (CVC Coaches) with training sessions that include short podcasts, short readings, and conversation guides.
>
> It's exciting as I walk the halls of CVC on Sunday mornings to see our offices populated with leadership development huddles. We

offer three services on Sunday morning. So, it's not uncommon to see one of the hours used for leadership development. Staff members who are busy in other ministries are giving up their offices to our volunteers on Sundays. LifeGroup leaders gather with their coaches so that laughing, learning, and loving take place. There's nothing quite as fulfilling as stepping back and watching leaders you've trained lead well. Creating a dynamic, comprehensive, unifying, and empowering Leadership Pipeline is a surefire way to make sure that your impact will be bigger than you![2]

Churches can hyperfocus on the pain points within their ministry areas and attempt to develop leadership culture from the bottom up. But a leadership development culture requires churches to start at the point of influence and not at the point of pain, which is exactly what Rick has done so effectively. Unfortunately, attempts to create culture from the bottom up rarely work. However, if you start from the top— from the primary leader and influencer in the church—it is far more likely that a leadership culture will flow down. Over time, the values of the leader will become the values of the organization, so pastors and senior leadership must do whatever is necessary to prioritize leadership development and call others to follow the model they've set. Their examples will help shape a culture of leadership development in the church.

8

Expect Leadership Development

We're aiming for a church culture that says, "Discipling leaders is what we do!" It must be stated clearly for people to get it. But stating it clearly is still not enough. You must make decisions that give evidence that leadership development is a high value in your organization.

The best way to do this is to make leadership development a part of the job description for every key leader. This expectation will likely be met with resistance, at least at the outset, for several reasons.

First, some leaders will feel threatened by the process and worry that they will no longer be needed. The language we use for leadership development often, perhaps unintentionally, communicates this reality. You might hear a senior leader telling a staff person or key lay leader that they need to "replace" themselves. This challenge sounds like a step in the right direction, but it can heighten the fear many feel. They don't want to be replaced, so they don't develop leaders. It's far more effective to challenge leaders to "reproduce" themselves—by finding two or three other people who can do what they do.

Other leaders resist the notion of leadership development because they have a fear of letting go. Many have a personal standard of excellence and fear that if they empower other leaders and delegate certain functions, the quality of the ministry will suffer. This forces us to consider what we value most. If your value of excellence overrides your value for leadership development, then you will never hand off key responsibility. However, if the value of leadership development trumps that of excellence, then you will create a culture where failure is acceptable, safe, and expected. It's a delicate balance, but when leaders are put in key roles, they should be given the freedom to *grow* into excellence rather than being expected to attain that from the outset.

Finally, many will push back on the notion of leadership development because they feel inadequately trained to do so. I'll often give churches an exercise to illustrate this point. Imagine that a leader is given a simple scale with numbers ranging from 1 to 10, with 1 being low and 10 being high. The leader is then asked to circle the number that indicates their perceived capability in developing leaders. This score would give a clear picture of how qualified a leader felt for the tasks of developing others. Then, using the same scale, the leader is asked to put an *X* on the number that indicates the current level of expectation they feel in their role for developing leaders. This mark indicates the pressure the leader feels to make other leaders based on their role and function.

For the sake of discussion, Steve puts a circle around the number 3 and an *X* through the number 7. This is a problem. Steve feels like he's expected to develop leaders but lacks the training or confidence to accomplish the task. Steve likely feels shame and guilt for his failure. Sarah, on the other hand, puts a circle around 7 and an *X* through 3. Her issue is the opposite. She feels highly capable of producing other leaders but feels like her job and church culture do not value or expect her to accomplish this task. Neither Steve nor Sarah will likely disciple leaders, though their reasons are quite different.

In many ways, the rest of this book is an attempt to address Steve's issue. If he's reading this book (and surely there's some Steve who is!), then I hope to provide the tools necessary for him to grow in confidence. Sarah's issue is, in many ways, an easier fix. The culture must change so that leadership development is normative and expected.

Building this goal into a leader's job description is the place to begin. All leaders should have an expectation that they will invest the time, effort, and energy required to develop others. They should be free to invest in this work and celebrated when they take steps in the right direction.

James Griffin, pastor of Crosspoint City Church in Cartersville, Georgia, and Suzy Jordan, Crosspoint's executive pastor, went through the Leadership Pipeline training a couple of years ago. There was great enthusiasm in their team about the process when they went through the training, but once the training was over and it was time to implement these ideas, they found themselves distracted by the day-to-day whirlwind of ministry activity.

Suzy noticed that some staff took off strong and began implementing the plan while others did not. It was evident that some of the staff were still struggling, believing that this was just one more program or one more thing they had to do. Her driving passion was to create a culture that prioritized developing leaders. As she saw some of the staff waning in their commitment to building a leadership development culture, she told James it was time to reinforce this value and get the troops fired up about leadership development again.

As they discussed the challenges, James pulled the staff together to let them know that leadership development was not optional. He reminded them of the tremendous growth the church had experienced, the great impact they were having, and that the only way they were going to continue this level of impact was by taking the Leadership Pipeline seriously. He understood that perhaps not everyone was cut out to develop leaders, so he told his staff, if they didn't like developing leaders, or it just didn't fit their gifting, then that was fine, but they just couldn't remain on staff and the church would help them find another job that fit their giftings.

From that day on, those who were killing it, killed it even more. Those who didn't have traction began to get traction. The ones not on board realized what they were going to have to do. Suzy began to meet weekly with those who were struggling to give them clarity, to cheer them on, and to coach them. She told me, "if the lead pastor isn't behind it, you don't need to try doing the Leadership Pipeline." And she's right.

9

Fight for It

If you've led a church for any length of time, you've heard a variety of excuses. We, as leaders, are prone to make some excuses ourselves. This is particularly true when it comes to the issue of leadership development. It's one thing that we all know we should be doing but never seem to get around to making happen. For leadership development to become a normative culture, we must ruthlessly fight against the common excuses people give for not doing it.

The excuses for an inability to develop leaders are common to every area of ministry. Perhaps the most common is to blame a lack of time. We are so busy—consumed with an assortment of responsibilities and pressures, from both our churches and our homes. Our schedules testify to the reality that most leaders are maxed out.

But instead of being a reason to not develop leaders, busyness should cause us to prioritize this work. Our lack of time is all the evidence we need of the necessity for leadership development. Perhaps if we were to make this more important than other things, we would have more time to do what only we can do. Also, the busier you are, the more opportunity a potential leader has to watch you in action, and the greater the likelihood you can delegate a few responsibilities to those you are developing.

Another excuse is simply not knowing how to develop leaders. Because a legitimate plan for leadership development is rare, many of those in leadership positions have had no clear training for how to go about developing other leaders. As a result, they lack the confidence to begin to even make an attempt. Yet this reality should motivate a leader to work even harder to design a plan so that future leaders have the benefit of a clear blueprint to follow. In today's information age, there are plenty of tools designed to help you grow as a leader developer. If we say we don't know how to develop leaders, then we're admitting that either we're lazy or it's not important enough to figure out.

Some will give the excuse that they don't see the need for making leadership development a priority. Within their current church structure, they seem to have all the leaders necessary to execute their mission. In these situations, the fact that all current leadership positions are filled means that no one is thinking about the recruitment, training, and development of future leaders. The shortsighted nature of this excuse is clear. Leadership development is built around a vision of what could be in the future and not simply designed to meet the current ministry needs. Leaders who do not reproduce other leaders ultimately damage the long-term health of their organization. A refusal to reproduce leaders is one of the most selfish behaviors a leader can exhibit.

The flip side of this excuse is that in many churches the current leader does not believe anyone is ready to be developed—or at least they may not know of anyone who is raising their hand and asking to be developed. But the fact that we do not know of anyone wanting to be developed does not mean that no such person exists. The first leaders Jesus developed, His disciples, weren't exactly begging for someone to develop them. Jesus took a risk on people. He asked them to assume a role, to get involved, to make an entry-level commitment. He didn't recruit Matthew, Peter, and Andrew and send them out immediately to share the gospel with the world. Instead He got them on His team and started working with them to take their next steps. Jesus saw the potential in this ragtag group of men and invested in them in such a way that they revolutionized the world.

Those who do sense a compelling need for leadership development may still fail to create an effective system because they use the excuse that the church lacks the financial resources to develop leaders. While money is certainly important for the mission of the church, it doesn't take money to develop leaders—at least not money spent in the ways we typically invest our resources. Yes, it would take money (and lots of it) to send all our leaders to conferences or design seminars to train these men and women, but it doesn't take money for one leader to invest in a reproducible, relational process designed to foster leadership development. If you are looking for a downloadable model, it will cost you and your church money, but if you really want to develop people, money shouldn't be a concern.

A final excuse—and perhaps an underlying reason behind the excuses already mentioned—is a bit more sinister. Many leaders fail to develop others because of *pride*. They like to be needed. They sense a certain level of fulfillment when everything revolves around them. They worry about what might happen if others are better at a certain task than they are. So for this reason they resist empowering others to lead. I have noticed in my own ministry journey there are times my identity gets too tightly tied to my ministry. And when my identity is dependent on my role in ministry that is a dangerous place to be. I begin to use my ministry activity to fuel my sense of worth. Leadership development requires a sense of humility, and those with this type of humility will willingly and enthusiastically identify the gifts and talents of others and empower them to live out their calling, even when it means they are more gifted than yourself. If you are not identifying and developing others, then it may be good to pause and ask if there is a sense of pride that is keeping you from empowering others to lead.

People make dozens of excuses for not developing leaders. And each of these excuses points to genuine challenges related to leadership development: we struggle to find time, we wonder if we have what it takes to develop another person, we question the adequacy of our resources, and we battle with the pride that easily entangles our lives.

We all face these challenges. Churches who are doing a poor job with leadership development face them, and churches who are doing a great job with leadership development face them. It's not the challenges that determine whether you're successful with leadership development. The challenges are the same in every church. If you are the key leader, then it is your job to work to fight these excuses and shape an alternative narrative to turn these excuses into action. It's how you address them that matters. But we find in most cases it's the challenges that become excuses, and the excuses paralyze the leaders to the point that they don't even try. Those who push through the excuses and fight for leadership development culture are poised to take the next step to develop a structure that fosters this unified goal.

Take a few minutes and think through the excuses you and your team use for not developing more leaders. List those excuses in a journal and consider what action steps you need to take to fight to eliminate them.

Part 3

Structure

Organize an Aligned Leadership Structure
That Clarifies a Development Pathway

10

Structure
Matters

I was in the gym a few years ago when I loaded a small amount of weight to do a set of warm-up squats. Once I secured myself under the bar, I went down for my first rep.

That's when I felt something pop and found myself crashing to the ground in pain. Fortunately, the Smith machine caught the weight, but I could tell I was in trouble. I hobbled out of the gym and made my way to the chiropractor who informed me that the lack of warm-up and the amount of weight stressed my spine, and it was now significantly out of alignment. I wasn't going to need surgery, but I was going to be immobile for a while. He was right; it was a full week before I was able to walk and about two weeks before my back was finally back into full alignment.

Just as our spinal structure can dramatically impact our mobility, the structure of your church can have serious impact on your ability to effectively move the vision of your church forward. Churches can diminish their impact because their structure is undefined, misaligned, or confusing. As a result, churches limp along, trying to make progress on the mission and find the leaders necessary to keep the church moving forward.

When we look at our world, we see that everything God created has a structure. So why wouldn't the church? Besides, didn't He use the body as a word picture for the church? And doesn't the body have a very defined, intentional structure?

Structure impacts how fluid and mobile your church is in moving people into postions that match their calling and leadership potential. Many people may struggle with this concept of making structure such a priority. It feels like we are trying to focus too much on business or corporate principles and ignoring the spiritual aspect of church health. But the truth is, structure isn't just a business concept, it's also a vital spiritual principle. The structure of your church can be a very serious spiritual matter. When a pastor ignores the practical importance of structure, it can result in spiritual problems like diminished energy, impact, and spiritual growth.

Diminished Energy

After accepting the call to lead the Hebrew people out of Egypt, Moses found himself in the middle of the desert—overwhelmed by the demands of ministering to people. When his father-in-law, Jethro, came to visit, he made an observation that dramatically impacted Moses' leadership. We see the story in Exodus 18:14–18:

> When his father-in-law saw all that Moses was doing for the people, he said, "What is this you are doing for the people? Why do you alone sit as judge, while all these people stand around you from morning till evening?" Moses answered him, "Because the people come to me to seek God's will. Whenever they have a dispute, it is brought to me, and I decide between the parties and inform them of God's decrees and instructions." Moses' father-in-law replied, "What you are doing is not good. You and these people who come to you will only wear yourselves out. The work is too heavy for you; you cannot handle it alone."

Jethro saw that Moses was pushing himself beyond reasonable limits to meet the demands of ministry. The solution he gave wasn't to pray more or take a day off. His advice was to build a healthy structure so that he could lead the nation in a way that guarded and sustained everyone's health.

Do you ever find it difficult to get out of bed, put on your leadership hat, and face another day at the office? All of us have had those days where we find ourselves unable to focus, lead with passion, or steward the vision because we're emotionally drained. If you find yourself working too hard and too long, it could be time to look at the structure of your church.

Diminished Impact

The passage we've already considered in Acts 6 illustrates the challenges of diminished impact. Can you imagine if the leaders of the Jerusalem church had simply said, "We really don't care if some widows are being neglected. We've got too much on our hands already to deal with issues like that"?

Not only would this lack of love have been a lack of compassion but the apostles would have missed a God-given opportunity for impact. These widows were real people with real needs that the church had the power to address. All it needed to do was work to create a structure that would serve these widows well and make sure they were not overlooked.

But notice the apostles' solution. They could have easily said, "Hey, there are twelve of us and twelve months in a year. Let's set up a monthly rotation among us to take care of these widows." Instead of becoming the solution to the problem and doing it themselves, they strengthened the structure of the church by having the people designate leaders to take care of this need.

When churches experience growth, the existing team often resorts to working harder and longer. Then the pastor finds himself bewildered as he is celebrating the great things God is doing while mourning the simultaneous loss of key team members who are burning out. Establishing a healthy structure based on your vision can help eliminate these challenges.

Diminished Spiritual Growth

We learn from Titus 1 that Paul and Titus led a successful evangelistic campaign on the island of Crete—a culture of people known to be liars and lazy. However, the gospel had taken root, and now there were new believers all over the island. Paul had to move on, but he left his companion Titus behind. Knowing there was a high risk that these new believers might fall away, Paul instructed Titus to establish a structure to support the spiritual growth of the newly founded churches. He wrote, "The reason I left you in Crete was that you might put in order what was left unfinished and appoint elders in every town, as I directed you" (v. 5).

Healthy structures support the spiritual development of the people in your church. Establishing ministry leaders, group leaders, or missional community leaders is all a part of making disciples through the ministry of your church. But if you don't identify the type of structure you need for the growth of your church, then spiritual development may suffer.

These problems heighten the need for a clear leadership structure in the church. The remainder of this part will be spent discussing how we might go about creating a structure that makes leadership development a natural outcome of the church's mission.

11

The Problem of
Misalignment

When working with a church to help build their leadership development strategy, one of the first exercises we do helps them get a good picture of the health of their structure. We ask each department to take a giant wall Post-it and draw the structure of their area. We give specific instructions not to draw what they want it to be but to draw their current reality, showing the levels, the title of each position, and also the ratios of how many people report to each leader.

After everyone finishes we put all the Post-its on one wall stacked next to each other. The staff gathers, steps back, and looks at all the structures together. We tell them they are looking at a giant X-ray of the structure of their church. Then we ask them to think of themselves as an organizational chiropractor and tell us what problems they see in this X-ray of their church structure. What needs to be adjusted?

We rarely have to say much. They immediately begin to spout out the problems they see. Looking at the current reality of their structure visually makes the problem obvious. Here are the typical mistakes I see in most organizational structures that hinder their leadership development efforts.

Unhealthy Span of Care

One mistake I often see is a structure with a ratio of too many people reporting to one person. The span of care is too large. One person can't have twenty direct reports in a leadership structure. I know, because I've tried it, and I almost burned myself out. I remember the angst on the face of a children's pastor at a recent training I conducted. She was visibly shaken by something, so I asked her to tell me what it was. She simply said, "I'm overwhelmed." Then she showed me her structure, which indicated she had 110 leaders reporting directly to her. It's no wonder she described herself as stressed, overworked, and overwhelmed. Who wouldn't?

Misaligned Terminology

Another mistake that can create confusion is teams using different terminologies for the various levels of leadership rather than aligning the terminologies at every level for every ministry. A church I was coaching had three ministries that used different terms for those who were leading their leaders. The groups ministry called them "shepherds," the children's ministry called them "coordinators," and the first impressions ministry called them "coaches." We will be more effective if we align the language of what we call leaders at various levels. Without such alignment it's difficult to have a clear developmental pathway through which you can disciple your leaders.

No Structure for Development

Then there are those churches that put together a structure simply thinking of who reports to who. Sure, this helps create clear lines of communication. But rarely do they go beyond that and think about what a leadership development pathway in their church would look like—the Leadership Pipeline. In other words, it is common for a church structure to have clarity of function, but it's rare for a church to make sure their structure creates clarity for development as well.

Creating a structure that is designed for developing and discipling leaders at various levels will help you and those you lead discover a whole new set of possibilities for leaders in your church.

Taken together, these structural problems compound the general challenge related to leadership development in the church. Regardless of what good plans we may have in mind, if we do not first and foremost create a clear and compelling structure, then our plans will never come to fruition.

How about you? How aligned is your leadership structure? Do the following exercise with your team to find out. Have each ministry draw the structure of their area reflecting the current reality. When they draw it, have them label the title of each role as well as the ratios of people reporting to each other. For example, you may have a student director who has forty-one small-group leaders who report to him, while also having fourteen team member volunteers who help him with hospitality. That means this one student director has a total of fifty-five people who report directly to him.

Then compare the structures of each ministry. What did you discover? What was confusing? What needs to be changed?

For example, Kelli Wommack, leadership development pastor at Christ Community Church in Columbus, Georgia, faced a significant pain point. The church had recently moved into a new building, and they were growing exceptionally fast. The staff was overworked, weary, and tired because they were trying to lead their areas, recruit volunteers, grow large teams, and train others as best as they could. In addition, the staff was trying to care for the souls of those they led. This meant that many were singlehandedly overseeing teams of fifty to one hundred members. The staff's ratios were out of whack, and staff and team members were discouraged, which made retention of team members difficult.

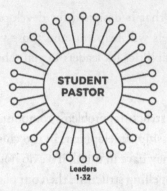

Leaders
1-32

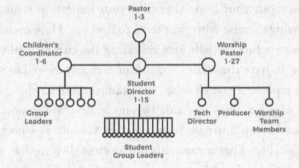

Christ Community's work on the Leadership Pipeline helped them align ministry teams, titles, and roles, and establish healthy leadership ratios. Now they are not caring for teams of fifty to one hundred but lovingly leading just the level of leaders directly below them. Soul care now occurs with eight to ten people, which makes the entire process manageable. Kelli said, "We have hired mostly within as our goal is to develop leaders into coaches, coaches into directors, and directors into pastors. If we hire from within, we don't have to train someone in our culture and values, and we are able to focus on task development."[1]

The alignment in Christ Community is now producing an abundant harvest of reproducing leaders. Now that we've identified misalignment, let's focus on bringing a healthy alignment to your leadership structure.

12

Aligning Your Structure

Imagine a twenty-one-year-old college student walks into your office and says he wants to plant a church in the future. His question is not, "How do I get the appropriate education?" He wants to get the proper experience in the context of your church so that he can be sent out one day to plant a church. Imagine the benefit if you had a learning experience that would help him develop the necessary leadership character, competencies, and experience in sequential order. What pathway would you prescribe for him to develop the skills to become a church planter? We could apply the same question to any role within your local church ministry—children's ministry, worship, or any other role in which you need more leaders. Developing a clear structure will help you make significant progress in developing the leaders you need. The place to begin is to make sure that you have clear definitions of your structure. So, what do we do?

Leadership Pipeline

In 2004, I went on staff as leadership development pastor at Seacoast Church, a fast-growing, multisite church based in Mount Pleasant, South Carolina. On my first day, Pastor Greg Surratt gave me the book *The Leadership Pipeline* by Ram Charan, Steve Drotter, and Jim

Noel.[1] This book had a profound impact on the way I look at leadership development.

One of its greatest contributions is helping leaders think through a practical structure for the development of other leaders.

During Charan's time at GE, he was influenced by the teaching and concepts of Walt Mahler. Mahler had developed a concept he called Crossroads that described a pathway by which organizations could develop future leaders for every level of their organization. Later Charan innovated on these concepts and wrote the book *The Leadership Pipeline*, and the concept caught on.[2]

While the book had a great impact on me, it used very technical business language and was targeted to large, international corporations. I present church leaders with a generic Leadership Pipeline model that takes Charan's concepts and adjusts them to fit the local church context. In simple terms, the Leadership Pipeline model presupposes that every organization has a variety of levels of leadership. These levels make up a progressive pathway you can use to develop new leaders. The pipeline lays out a natural progression for those who are called and have the competency to move to higher levels of leadership. This concept is so fundamental to the theme of this book that I've chosen to capitalize the two words throughout when referencing it.

The descriptions below are what I call generic Leadership Pipeline terms. They are generic in the sense that they describe the scope of leadership of each level. Later we will look at how to turn the generic language into specific terms for each level.

The first level is *leading self*. In the local church context, this is someone who is in the basic discipleship process. Perhaps they are simply attending church or maybe they've gotten involved in a small group or ministry team.

The next level is *leading others*. Once someone has learned to lead themselves, the next step is to take on leading a small team or group of people.

The third level is *leading leaders*. Now that the leader has mastered the skills of leading a team, they can begin to lead a small team of leaders.

The fourth level is *leading a ministry area*. This means the leader is now ready to provide visionary leadership for a ministry area with oversight of those who are leading leaders.

The fifth and final level is *leading the church*. This is an individual or a team of people who provide visionary oversight of the church as a whole.

Churches may need fewer or more levels depending on the size of the church. Now let's go back to our ambitious twenty-one-year-old and see how an aligned Leadership Pipeline structure can assist you in discipling him as a future church planter.

Lead Self

The first step in this developmental pathway would be for him to learn to lead himself. You might be tempted to assume this step, but we've all seen in the evangelical landscape of North America the unfortunate consequences of elevating someone in leadership without a corresponding maturity in character. You should recommend that he engage in group life in your church and begin to learn the basics of discipleship so he can lead himself well. Next, he decides to join your small group, and you begin closely discipling him. Twelve months later, you see tremendous growth in this young man and an obvious calling into leadership.

Lead Others

Now that he is leading himself well, you recommend he move to the second step of leading others. You challenge him to start leading a small group of students so that he can gain experience in leading and influencing others in their spiritual development.

During the next two years you watch him effectively disciple and influence a small group of high school boys. As he grows, you challenge him to begin to lead a group of adults just as he did with the high school boys. Over the next year, you're amazed as he not only leads a college-age small group but also multiplies two groups out of his group. He is now showing evidence that he has the calling and capacity to lead at the next level of the Leadership Pipeline.

Lead Leaders

This young man is now twenty-six years old. He has finished college, is happily married with a child on the way, and is working full-time at a local bank near the church. You invite him to lunch and share the strengths and calling you see on his life. You praise him for growing the people in his group spiritually while also raising up new leaders and multiplying new groups. You invite him to the next step on the Leadership Pipeline: leading leaders. You ask him to provide coaching oversight for five of the college-age small groups in the church. This would involve meeting with the leaders and providing encouragement, ongoing training, and troubleshooting.

During the next two years you provide him with books and resources to help him grow even deeper spiritually. You meet with him regularly as his mentor. You see him skyrocket in his spiritual leadership skill and influence both in the church and at home with his wife and now two children. You recognize he has a godly love for not just his own family but several families in the church with whom he and his wife have close relationships. They often seek out his guidance on marital and parenting issues. You encourage him in this and provide him with a reading list of marriage and family resources and training conferences he can consider. He takes to it enthusiastically.

Lead a Department

During the past few years your church has grown. Now you need to add a staff person to oversee the family ministry department. You know this young man is the right person for the job. Once again, you meet with him and praise the progress he's made. You invite him to take the next step on his spiritual leadership journey: leading a department. He readily agrees, and you bring him on board your staff to provide visionary oversight and leadership of the family ministry. During his five years on staff, you give him a variety of challenges: increasing leadership responsibility, preaching opportunities, and many chances to follow beside you in some tough ministry situations.

Lead an Organization

You aren't surprised when a few years later the young man walks into your office and announces he feels a definite call to plant a new church. Your immediate reaction is that you don't want to lose him! However, you also know it's not about you and growing your church. It's about God and expanding His kingdom. So, you affirm the strengths you've seen in him and confirm that he is ready for the final step in the Leadership Pipeline: leading an organization.

Defining your Leadership Pipeline

For a church to have strong alignment in their structure, they have to determine their levels and language of their Leadership Pipeline. I recommend identifying how many levels you need for your church. While it may sound like this concept is only for large churches, I have worked with more small churches (50 to 200 members) than large churches, helping them through this very process.

The size of your pipeline will be determined by the size of your church. Smaller churches (30 to 250 people) usually need three to four levels in their pipeline. Larger churches (250 to 1,000 people) generally will need four to five levels in their pipeline. Churches above 1,000 in attendance will usually need five to six levels in their pipeline, and churches above 5,000 in attendance may have up to seven levels in their pipeline. I always advise not to have more than seven.

Once the church determines the number of levels needed, then they begin to name each level. The first thing I have them do is label each level and write a description of the scope of leadership for that level. A five-level Leadership Pipeline would look like the chart below.

- **Senior Leader:** Provides visionary leadership and shapes the culture of the overall church. (Lead Organization)
- **Director:** Provides visionary leadership over a specific area of ministry with oversight of coaches. (Lead Department)
- **Coach:** Leads a small team of leaders to provide further equipping, encouragement, and evaluation. (Lead Leaders)
- **Leader:** Leads a small team of people in a specific area of ministry. (Lead Others)
- **Team Member/Participant:** Serves on a ministry team or participates in a group. (Lead Self)

Gather your team and discuss how many levels seem appropriate for your church and what the common terminology could possibly be for each level. One of the most important steps in this segment is writing a description of the scope of responsibility for each level. Describing the scope of responsibility is in part how you decide what level a leader is functioning at in your church.

I was working with a church one time who determined to call those overseeing ministry areas their "directors." According to their description, a director was one who provided visionary oversight of a particular ministry with coaches reporting to them. One of their staff had the title of communication director. But it became clear to her and the pastor that functionally she was operating at a coach level. She had a small team of people with two leaders under her ministry. When we discussed this with her, she was excited to hear that she was empowered to raise up more leaders and coaches in her ministry area. She told us, "The level of excellence was so high here that I didn't think I was allowed to empower others at such a high level of leadership." Within a year she had built out a full Leadership Pipeline and was now truly functioning as a director.

Go to www.multiplicationeffect.com/structure to download the structure worksheet to help you define the Leadership Pipeline for your church.

13

Establish Healthy Spans of Care

I was standing with a church staff in front of a wall filled with Post-it notes showing the current reality of each department's structure. There was almost an audible groan as they looked at their structure on the wall. Their words matched their posture: "We are a mess." One of the young pastors pulled me over to his chart during the break and asked me to analyze it with him.

I used this as an opportunity to help him diagnose the issue. I asked, "What level of care are you providing for these leaders? What level of coaching are you providing for them? How effective do you feel you're being in helping them accomplish their mission?" He admitted he was feeling like a failure on all counts. But when I asked him what he could do about it he responded, "I don't have a choice. I have to lead this many—there's no one else to do it."

I see many directors who have a span of care ratio of 1 to 35 or 1 to 50, and in every case they feel overwhelmed and believe they are failing those they lead. When there is a large span of care, I typically see the following problems.

People Don't Feel a Part of a Team

Having too many people you're responsible for makes it difficult to communicate effectively. As a result, people begin to feel like cogs in a machine rather than valued members of a team. They can feel under-appreciated over time. Certain ministries, like children's ministry, may have a predetermined, state-mandated ratio of adults to kids, but it's wise that other ministries self-impose a ratio restriction to promote effective team function.

People Don't Get Coaching

In cases of large ratios, these leaders get little to no feedback on what they're doing well or how they could grow in their leadership. They are placed in a spot with minimal instruction, and the leader above them hopes for the best. Rather than being developed for their task, some end up feeling ineffective or guilty over their failures and are likely to simply give up.

People Don't Get Stuff Done

Poor ratios lead to ineffective work. Ideas and tasks bottleneck with a few key leaders, often awaiting a meeting or decision from a supervisor that seems to never happen. If healthy ratios are in place, people are freed to communicate more effectively and work together in collaborative relationships, and the overall burden on the staff decreases.

People Don't Get Care

There's simply no way to maintain relational connection with a ratio of 1 to 75 or even 1 to 20. No leader has the bandwidth to care for that many people. Not only will the people grow isolated but the leader will likely know that he or she is simply not there for people. There will be a nagging sense that the leader is just not involved in people's lives enough to do the hard work of soul care. Even the great leaders in Israel—men like David and Hezekiah—needed others like Nathan and Isaiah who knew them well enough to challenge them spiritually and encourage them to persevere.

Several years ago I was studying Jesus' leadership development approach and John 15:15 stood out to me as a key passage. It is near the end of Jesus' earthly ministry, and He looked at His disciples and said, "I no longer call you servants . . . Instead, I have called you friends, for everything that I learned from my Father I have made known to you." That verse grabbed me: "I have called you friends." There is a popular teaching that says, "Don't get close to those you lead." But Jesus considered the men on His team to be friends.

And here's why this is so important: *your leadership development efforts will have greater impact when your leaders realize you're emotionally invested in them.* Smaller, healthy ratios help you connect more and more deeply with those you lead.

So you want to take a close look at the levels of your pipeline and ask yourself, *What would a healthy ratio of leader to team member be? What about a healthy ratio for coach to leader? Director to coach?* Once you identify your ratios, you will know how many leaders you have and how many leaders you need at each level.

Visit www.multiplicationeffect.com/structure to see a sample and download a worksheet to determine healthy ratios for your area of ministry.

14

Help People Identify
Their Next Step

Clear definitions help those in our system in understanding where they are now and what next steps would be logical. In my thirty-plus years of ministry, I have had many people approach me telling me God spoke to them and was calling them to be in ministry or plant a church. The Leadership Pipeline has been a significant help in guiding our conversation.

My first question is, "Where are you currently serving?" I want to discover if they are serving and growing in the basics of discipleship. From there I show them the pipeline and try to diagnose at what level of the pipeline they are currently leading. Based on where they place themselves, I can then help them see clearly the next step in the process. It's common for those who aspire to lead a ministry department or be a church planter to push back on the process. "You mean that I have to go through each of these steps before I can plant a church or lead a department?" they ask. The clear implication is that they think they should be able to opt out of certain steps or they resent the long timeline that is required to take these steps in order.

Skipping Levels

As you can see from the example from chapter 12, there was a logical progression of growth for our young leader. Each progressive step through the pipeline is essential to get to the next level. Skipping levels only undermines the development of your leader.

Several years ago I created a Church Planter Assessment, which is now the Send Network Assessment for the North American Mission Board. In this two-day assessment retreat, a team of people study a candidate's online profile and then interview them and have them go through a series of exercises meant to see whether this person is ready to plant a church. One of the key things we look for in these church planters is their leadership experience. I have seen many young leaders come through this assessment with a strong passion to plant a church, which would equate to leading the organization level of the pipeline. But as we interview them, we discover some have never even led a team (lead others), and some have never led leaders or led a department. In these cases, we always recommend that they slow their plans for planting a church to gain more experience at the different levels.

I see the same thing when I am consulting with churches. Many times, in the middle of the process, staff members admit they are over their heads because they were moved from leading themselves to leading a department. Their lack of experience and training cause them to struggle with the role. One of the best things we can do for future leaders is help them work through a logical progression of growth and development as a leader.

Not everyone will walk his or her way through every level of the Leadership Pipeline. In fact, if you try to push people through the pipeline, you've misunderstood the intent of the pathway. The Leadership Pipeline is not designed to move as many people up as possible. It is simply a structured pathway that helps you move those who have the calling to a greater scope of leadership responsibility. So how do we know who and when to move people into the next level of leadership?

There are five critical transition factors that must be considered at each turn in the pipeline. If these are overlooked or ignored, you will undermine the full development of those you're putting into leadership. So, as you consider developing someone to another level, look at each of these factors.

Calling—Do they have the calling to lead at the next level? Make sure you've given them a season to pray regarding God's calling on their life and whether or not God is calling them to lead at that next level.

Competency—Do they understand the competencies needed to lead at the next level? Part of your job in discipling them to the next level will be to define what competencies are needed at that level and equip them to lead well.

Commitment—Do they understand the higher level of commitment needed to lead at the next level? Before you start training them, make sure they understand the scope of the responsibility and expectations for the new role.

Core Values—Can they embody the core values of the organization at a deeper level? As one moves up the Leadership Pipeline, they must embrace and embody the values of the organization at a level that calls others to follow in a unique way. The more leadership responsibility, the greater the burden that the leader is replicating the organization's DNA.

Character—Do they have the character necessary to lead at the next level? With each move up the Leadership Pipeline there are greater temptations with pride, power, and prestige. You must work with them to understand the character requirements at each level.

I was working with a multisite church that had a pastor who had skipped from small-group leader to campus pastor, which was a big jump on any Leadership Pipeline. After a couple of years he had to be transitioned to a different role because he was unable to lead the campus well. But ultimately it wasn't his fault. The senior leaders of the church saw that he was a man who loved Jesus and was growing in his faith, so they placed him in that role. But he had skipped important levels and it undermined the natural flow of development for him. The loving and kind thing to do is to help people identify the appropriate next step.

15

Develop for Vision, Not for Need

How many leaders do you currently have serving your mission? Is it enough? How many additional leaders do you need? These are important questions to consider if we want to build a culture of leadership development.

Consider for example a student director who oversees a student ministry of thirty students and five leaders. She knows it's wise to have one leader for every six students. And she feels comfortable they are at that ratio in their ministry. But then one of her leaders suddenly moves out of state. If you were to ask her how many leaders she needs, she would likely answer one. Realizing she needs a new leader, she works to find someone to fill the vacant role. Upon finding a new leader she then stops thinking about leadership development and goes back to doing the other aspects of her role that keep her occupied week to week. This is what I call developing for *need*.

Developing for *vision* necessitates looking for enough leaders to fit what you need based upon your vision for growth. Consider the same scenario but this time the student director has an understanding that she needs to be developing for vision. Instead of defining the student ministry by the thirty students who currently attend, she projects forward to the forty-five students she prays will be participating one year from now. As a result, instead of trying to find one leader to fill the gap she currently has, she is working with her team to develop three or four leaders for future growth. The focus on developing for vision helps your ministry be prepared with leaders before the growth happens.

When Paul was advising Timothy regarding leadership in the church of Ephesus, he gave him some critical instruction for the development of leaders. He wrote, "The things you have heard me say in the presence of many witnesses entrust to reliable people who will also be qualified to teach others" (2 Timothy 2:2). Paul's challenge was future oriented. He was advising Timothy to start a leadership development movement that would equip the church for future growth. In fact, this one verse contains four generations of multiplication! Paul understood that God was on the move and would continue to bring people to faith and into the church.

Timothy needed to be ready by continually raising up men who could equip others. That is developing for vision!

Here's the key: *you must have a vision for an ever-expanding pipeline of leaders.* Through this process, I've shown you how to define your pipeline. But in later chapters I will show you how to assess and fill your pipeline. Ultimately, you will be assessing the health of the pipeline in your area of ministry and taking responsibility for developing an abundant harvest of reproducing leaders under you. When we approach leadership development with this mentality, we have a better chance of developing a deep bench of leaders who are ready to help us as the church grows. But just having more leaders for our church isn't the primary goal. The ultimate goal of the Leadership Pipeline is to help churches establish a bench of leaders who can be sent out to start new churches or new campuses.

To develop leaders for vision and not just for need, I encourage churches to do the following exercise. First, identify how many leaders you currently have at each level of your pipeline. You've taken a first important step in the earlier chapter by determining healthy ratios for each level of your pipeline. Once that is in place, you project how many additional leaders you would need for each level if your church were to grow by 15 percent in the next year. Or you might even consider how many leaders you would need if you started a new campus or church in your community. This number becomes your leadership development goal for each ministry so that you are developing leaders for vision and not just need.

Todd Hampton, student pastor at Westridge Church, got serious about developing leaders after going through the Leadership Pipeline training. Little did he know that the student ministry he led would grow by 300 percent within just a few months. I was talking with Paul Richardson, the executive pastor at Westridge, and he told me, "I don't know what we would've done if Todd had not begun developing leaders in advance. In fact, I really believe that God brought the growth because we prepared the leaders."

What if God poured His favor on your ministry and it exploded by 15, 20, or even 30 percent? Would you have the leaders you needed to handle the growth? Why not start envisioning the growth and start developing leaders in preparation for it today?

Go to www.multiplicationeffect.com/structure and download the Have/Need worksheet to help you determine how many leaders you need at each level of your pipeline based on the anticipated growth of your church or ministry area.

Part 4

System

Design a Methodical System for Moving
Leaders Through the Leadership Pipeline

An Undefined System for Onboarding and Training Leaders

Most senior pastors I've met love to spend time thinking about the vision and mission of the church. But I've not met many who like to think about systems. And that is okay. I always tell them, "Your job is not to create systems, your job is to champion them." Most senior pastors get this and quickly understand that systems are a crucial part of having a healthy Leadership Pipeline. By systems, I'm referring to the processes that you use to bring people into the activity of leadership development and train them as they move through successive stages. Without a good system, churches leave their development efforts to chance, meaning their likelihood of success goes way down. A healthy pipeline that is flowing with effective, competent leaders has healthy systems that support it.

Several months ago I was having difficulty sleeping. I would wake up out of breath, gasping for air, with my chest hurting. I ignored it for a couple of days, hoping it would go away. But finally I grew concerned enough to go to the doctor. He ran a series of tests and discovered my lungs were filled with inflammation. I was fine during the day, but at night when I would lie down, the inflammation would fill my lungs, making it very difficult to breathe. When my respiratory system broke down, noticeable symptoms developed, and my health suffered.

Our bodies have more than ten systems that help them function in a healthy manner. The cardiovascular system circulates blood around the body through the heart, arteries, and veins. The digestive system processes the foods we eat and helps us absorb the essential nutrients we need for health and life. The muscular system enables us to move and accomplish tasks. When any of these systems is not functioning properly, we see and feel specific symptoms of a broken system.

In the same way, the effective function of a church requires certain systems. One of those systems is a leadership development system, which includes how you onboard and train leaders. Often, we have unhealthy leadership development results because an internal system is not functioning correctly. The symptoms range from a high turnover rate of volunteers to an inability to recruit enough people, a mismatch of gifts among those placed in various roles, or low morale among team members. These symptoms reveal that something is broken in our system.

I was reading an interview with Darren Patrick recently where he was asked, "Why do most churches stay small?" He responded,

> Largely because most pastors don't know how to build systems, structures, and processes that are not contingent upon them. Most pastors can care for people but don't build systems of care. Most pastors can develop leaders individually but lack the skill to implement a process of leadership development. When a pastor can't build systems and structures that support ministry, the only people who are cared for or empowered to lead are those who are "near" the pastor or those very close to the pastor. This limits the size of the church to the size of the pastor.[1]

He is right. Systems are critical.

Why do so many churches struggle to implement healthy systems? Many pastors, like those Patrick mentions above, feel they can do it themselves. There's no need for a system because everything rises and falls on a single, key leader. Others may say they are not a "systems person"—assuming that healthy systems depend on a certain personality type. Some may feel that systems take the place of the Holy Spirit in the process. And there are those who may claim to desire a more relational approach. They assume that a system is too rigid and will merely treat people like a cog in a giant machine.

But these objections are not necessarily true and, even if you say you don't want systems, every church has a system. The question is not whether you will have a system but whether you will have a good system or a bad one. Everything we do has steps involved. In many cases, systems emerge on their own because leaders have not taken the time to create an efficient or effective system that works. And when people struggle to move through our process, we're prone to blame them or the leader over them for their failure, when the real cause might be a broken system.

While there are many different systems to run a church, in this section we will focus on two that are essential to a healthy leadership development culture—a system for onboarding new leaders and a system for training new and existing leaders. By the end of this section you will have an aligned system that every ministry department can use for onboarding and training your leaders at every level.

Onboarding

As I have worked with various churches across North America, I have found that most of them have some sort of system for onboarding new team members but not leaders. For example, a church might have a process for onboarding someone to serve in the kid's ministry but has not defined the steps for moving that person into a role as a leader, coach, or director in that same ministry.

Staff members are left to their intuition for onboarding leaders, coaches, or others at higher levels of leadership. They simply assume that they will know how to promote others and that these people will naturally drift into these roles. Most often, that doesn't happen.

An intentional onboarding process can be a benefit to the potential new leader and add value to their development if done the right way. Affirmation of a person's call and fit into a leadership position is important because it protects the church and the individuals from being put in the wrong role. The onboarding process—if done correctly—can be an essential part of a church's discipleship process.

Training

Again, many churches have some sort of initial orientation training for new team members, but it is very rare for churches to have intentional training for those in higher levels of leadership. This causes the new leaders to experience unnecessary failures and frustrations. It leads to a loss of confidence and ultimately can cause the leader to mislabel themselves as a failure and drop out of leadership all together.

The Ridge Church in Milwaukee, Wisconsin, has experienced explosive growth under the church planter Mark Weigt. With the growth and the anticipation of adding a second location, they were beginning to feel the pain of a leadership shortage. Before going through the Leadership Pipeline process, their staff were not using a common system—in fact most didn't have a system for onboarding and training. As a result, they experienced frustration, overworked leaders, burnout, and disillusionment. They finally said "enough is enough" and worked through the pipeline process. During the Leadership Pipeline training, they designed a uniform system that each of their staff is now committed to use. Executive Pastor Jason Vanderpal recounted seeing leaders regain the fire in their eyes and passion in their voices because of the development and implementation of the pipeline. And imagine the relief when it came time to start their second campus that they had a defined Leadership Pipeline along with a system for onboarding and training the new leaders for that campus.

Having a clear, aligned system makes the onboarding and training experience better for both the new leader and the ministry department leader that oversees that area of ministry. In this section, we will learn how to design a methodical system for moving leaders through the Leadership Pipeline.

17

Diagnosing the System

Before we present some action steps to create a healthy system, it's important to diagnose the current reality in your church. Some of the previous experiences in this book have likely clued you in to some challenges already, but now consider someone in your church's leadership who is currently underperforming. Now let's ask some diagnostic questions:

- Did you screen them ahead of time by having them complete a questionnaire identifying their gifts, passions, personality, and past experiences?
- Did you give them a season to pray and observe the ministry in action before they stepped into leadership?
- Did you meet with them one-on-one to discuss the role and responsibilities?
- Did you give them a written role description and go over it with them?
- Did you provide training in the specific skills you expect for that role?
- Are you providing ongoing communication, support, and development?
- Are you providing feedback on their strengths and the areas in which they need to grow?
- Are you providing opportunities for peer-to-peer learning?

Most have not received this type of systematic onboarding and development. Is the core problem their skill or your system? It may be that their skill is inadequate for the role, but without a healthy system, you'll never know. A strong system is the only way to produce a strong leader.

The Big Picture

When I'm walking a church through the Leadership Pipeline process, I will ask them to imagine they walk into the office on Monday morning and there is a guest card in their inbox. The card indicates the person has been attending the church for about eight months and is now ready to serve on a ministry team. Then, I ask them to sketch out what they would do to bring this person onto a team. From there, I ask that they fast-forward one year and assume that the same individual now wants to transition into a higher level of leadership. Again, they are asked to write out how they would take this person through an intentional process to move to the next step. Twice more, I ask them to do the same process, if the person now wants to become a leader of leaders or a leader of an organization. The gaps and challenges are evident to everyone in the room. I then become a counselor—reminding the group that this is normal and that they can have hope that a broken system can be fixed.

Most churches have no clear map in place for the various ministries to move people through the levels of the Leadership Pipeline. Some have systems that are operating in silos, meaning that each ministry is using different approaches for onboarding. For example, I was working with a church one time and noticed that six different ministries all had a leadership application. As I was praising them for having this in place, it became clear that each was unaware of the others' applications. They had created these in a vacuum rather than working together and aligning what they were looking for in leaders. Various other issues—such as mismatched language or no clear process of oversight—emerge when leaders are forced to look at their church's system from the perspective of someone moving through the process.

As with the human body, a healthy system has remarkable implications for the vitality of the church. These benefits should motivate leaders to push through their frustrations with their current reality and work to take steps to improve.

Communicates Expectations for the Role

People rise to clear expectations, or they reveal that they do not have what it takes to lead at that level. A clear system shows people exactly what is expected at each step of the process, so that they don't aspire to a new role only to find that it far exceeds their calling or competency once they step into that position.

Assesses the Person's Fit for the Role

Systems give you a built-in mechanism to assess whether someone will be a good fit for a new role. The person who struggled to effectively lead and multiply a small group will not likely succeed as a church planter. The system itself will expose this reality clearly—both to you as the leader and to the person who wants to step into a new role.

Gives Clear Steps They Can Take to Step into the Role

A healthy system makes it clear what is needed to move from one level of leadership to the next. Rather than a vague aspiration to a position, now people can see clearly what they need to do if they want to move up to greater levels of leadership.

Indicates How the New Leader Will Be Trained

Finally, a clear system should demonstrate the training that is needed throughout the process. No one is a ready-made leader—we all need training to function effectively in new roles. Some may look at the various stages of leadership and fear they don't have what it takes to lead at the next level, so a clear system can reassure them that they will be trained at each step along the way.

Now that we see the challenges of a misaligned system and the benefits of a healthy system, it's time to take some practical steps to reshape our system for maximum effectiveness.

18

Align Your Onboarding System Across Every Department

To learn how your church brings on new leaders, imagine you take a tour around the various ministries of your church and ask the directors, "How do you integrate new people into your team?"

Your first stop is the children's director's office. When you ask how she onboards new leaders, she gives you a detailed process that includes filling out an application, conducting a personal interview, and shadowing a current leader. Next, you stop by the student director's office. His answer is more relational—he spends time getting to know people and plugs them into new roles once he knows their gifts and passions and finds an appropriate fit. The worship director confesses that it's difficult to get new people on the worship team. There is no formal process. Usually someone simply approaches her and says they have musical gifts and want to serve. From there, the director invites them to a rehearsal, assesses their abilities, and gives them a role based on their level of talent.

Finally, the groups director shares his frustration with his current system because he simply can't seem to retain leaders. Currently, he hears about potential new leaders and invites them to a four-hour learning lab on a Saturday morning where he explains the mission behind groups and the responsibility group leadership would entail. After the training, he places people in the new leader's group and tells the newly appointed leader to feel free to call him for coaching or help if anything ever comes up.

This is a picture of the misalignment I typically see in churches. What about your church? Would the same be true? If so, here's a great place to start. Start with a blank slate that simply lists the various levels of leadership you've already determined in the last section. You may have a level for team members, leaders, coaches, directors, and senior leaders. Imagine you were building from scratch and create an ideal onboarding process for each level of your pipeline. Consider the following steps as you begin to build your onboarding system.

Identify What's Working

It's likely that you're currently doing several things right. Look at the aspects of the system for each of your departments that are currently working. Identify the various factors that contribute to success in some departments and hinder it in others. Tease out the best practices—particularly if some of those are common between multiple ministries. It's also important that you discern the "why" behind the "what" here. Resist the temptation to merely identify the things that are working and press to understand why those systems are working and others are not.

Identify Your Gaps

When you stop and look at your current reality as a team, you will typically see steps that you should be taking but have been overlooking. It's important that you discern these gaps as a team—some people will see things that others may miss. Capture everyone's input and write down diverse observations, even if you question the validity of some of the gaps people may point out. Often you will find common themes that help you see clear breakdowns in your system.

Write Out a Step-by-Step Process

Then, take the unified feedback and seek to combine the things that are working and the details that would address the gaps. Attempt to define a simple system for onboarding that will work across every department in your church. This brainstorm can then be presented to those who lead in various areas of the church for feedback and refinement.

Now let me give you a hint that will make this easier and faster. Start by building your onboarding system for the team member level only. Work with your team to capture every step involved in onboarding. Then I recommend putting those in buckets, or bigger categories, like the sample I've provided online (see the URL at the end of the chapter). Here's why this is easier and faster. Once you create and refine your onboarding system at the team member level, you simply copy and paste it into the leader level and make the necessary changes that apply to that level of leadership. Then you copy and paste the leader onboarding system into your next level of the Leadership Pipeline and once again make the appropriate adjustments. Keep doing this until you get to the final level of your Leadership Pipeline.

Keep in mind that not all ministries will have the exact same steps as the others. But you can still create one document for all ministries to use. Simply notate with an asterisk anything that is an exception. For example, on the sample I've provided you see *audition for worship ministry. There will only be a few exceptions, so this will enable you to have one document that all ministries use to show your onboarding process.

Start Using It

Now that you're done building out your onboarding system, make sure everyone has a copy and starts using it as they onboard new leaders at each level of the church. One of the best ways to learn what works and what doesn't is to put the system on the road and see how it works. Don't be afraid to continue to refine the system as you begin to use it in onboarding actual individuals.

Once you're finished aligning your onboarding system, you'll experience three major benefits. First, you won't have to make new choices every time a new person needs to be integrated into a team. Every leader of every department will have a clear, concise plan to follow. Second, you'll reduce frustration—both for you and for those who want to serve. People are perceptive, and they notice when leaders are making things up along the way. A detailed system will make it plain that you've thought out the process and know what you are doing as you seek to integrate them into the life of the church. Finally, you'll increase accountability among your leaders. You will be able to see who is following the system and who is not. This will help you press the system into others and make sure they are implementing it well.

Several years ago, when I was serving at Seacoast Church, we took our executive team to Chick-fil-A headquarters to meet with their upper management to learn from them. Seacoast was expanding their multisite locations and was looking to learn from models outside of the church. The Chick-fil-A lead team was gracious and gave us an extensive, behind-the-scenes glimpse of how Chick-fil-A identifies, chooses, onboards, and equips their store operators. The Seacoast team came back inspired and full of ideas. It caused them to revamp their onboarding process for leaders. They got more detailed and intentional with the process. Byron Davis, former CEO of Fisher-Price, was one of those from Seacoast in the Chick-fil-A meeting. After making the upgrades to the onboarding system, anytime a new leader was added to a team, Byron would ask, "Did you Chick-fil-A that new leader?" We all knew exactly what he was talking about. He was making sure we were using the onboarding system we had all agreed to.

Go to www.multiplicationeffect.com/system to see a sample onboarding system.

19

Align Your Training System
Across Every Department

The onboarding process is only the beginning of the work of developing future leaders. From there, you must now train and equip these individuals to serve well in their various ministry responsibilities. Certainly, there is, and should be, training as a part of the onboarding process. But there must also be ongoing training throughout the various ministry tasks should you hope to have effective, vibrant leaders.

It's rare to find churches that take an intentional and strategic approach to training new or existing leaders. As a result, staff defaults to doing development the way they were developed. Unfortunately, most were trained as a leader the way my father-in-law trained his son to swim. When Kip was three years old, John took him out back and threw his son in the pool. After being thrown in the pool a few times, Kip was forced to learn to swim or else he would drown.

Many leaders in the church try to develop leaders this way. They throw people into the swimming pool of leadership and expect them to learn to lead. As a result, many leaders drown under the pressure of new leadership responsibilities. They get overwhelmed and sink—many times leading to a reluctance to ever try to lead again.

They somehow make it to the side of the pool of leadership, crawl out, and say, "I'm never getting near the pool of leadership again!"

There are probably many reasons most leaders take the sink-or-swim approach to training new leaders. Those who make it after being thrown in the pool may assume that this is the way leadership development is meant to happen. Some simply replicate the process they experienced. Others have so much going on that they simply don't have time to develop a better process and do the painstaking work of equipping leaders over time. Sadly, this approach to leadership development has dangerous implications for the new leader and fails to provide a reproducible model that ensures the success of new leaders.

To counter this trend, it would be wise for a church to define a clear approach to training new leaders—one that could be used by all departments in a local church's ministry. You need to strive to design the way your church will develop leaders as a part of your system so that all those in leadership know that this is how leaders are developed in our place. This plan allows everyone to align and integrate a similar training process in every area of the church.

I've come to believe that a simple threefold process is best used to provide leadership training. This threefold process can be summarized using the words *prepare, equip,* and *inspire.*

Prepare

PRIMARY FOCUS: TRANSFORMATION

The *prepare* element in your leadership development strategy is what you do to get a potential leader ready for a new leadership role. In a later chapter I will show you three different approaches you can use to prepare potential leaders. Right now, I just want to give you the big picture.

The prepare portion of the leadership development strategy is designed to be a small training environment, usually no more than one on three, and is aimed at producing transformation in the life of a future leader. The preparation stage is designed to raise someone to the next level of your version of the Leadership Pipeline—from team member to leader, leader to leader of leaders, or leader of leaders to a leader of a department or an organization. The purpose of this training is to equip the new leader with the essential competencies that will be required in the new role. Many times, churches will give the new leader a job description or policies and procedures, but it's rare to see a church train the new leader in the actual competencies needed for the new role.

The method of training at this stage will be for an experienced leader to invest in a new leader. This type of training will typically happen every other week to give the new leader time to study and reflect on the concepts that are being discussed and try their hand at implementing some of the new ideas. This also provides a built-in shadowing process, whereby the future leader can watch the current leader apply these competencies in the fires of real-life ministry. This training is short, providing just enough time for the leader to make sure that the new leader feels confident and competent in what will be expected of them. Remember, the focus is not to simply give them information; rather we are taking a disciple-making approach to produce transformation in the individual's leadership competencies. This is why it is best to keep the prepare portion of the training restricted to a smaller handful of potential leaders.

Equip

PRIMARY FOCUS: COLLABORATION

The *equip* stage is designed for ongoing development with existing leaders. We will discuss this stage in more detail in a coming chapter, and I'll attempt to provide you with three different approaches for this level of training. What's important for now is that you grasp the general context for this level of training.

Typically, ongoing development takes place best in a team environment, with a team being as few as five people and as many as twelve. This type of training can work for all leaders, regardless of what level of the pipeline they currently serve. The main objective for this stage is to sharpen the leaders beyond the basic skills they needed at the outset of their service. The frequency of the training is typically once a month or in some cases once a quarter. The training is ongoing since the system is set up to help them continue to grow as a leader regardless of how long they've served in the past or how long they will serve in the future. The mode of training at this level is through peer-to-peer learning, where each leader collaborates with the others and contributes to the overall instruction of the team.

Inspire

PRIMARY FOCUS: INSPIRATION

The final stage is *inspiration*, where all leaders hear compelling vision designed to increase their momentum and fuel their zeal for the work. As with before, I'll wait until a coming chapter to discuss the details of this stage. At the outset, note that inspiration happens best in a large group setting, with one leader inspiring a large group. The purpose of the training is to inspire your leaders to keep going and keep growing. It's these large group trainings that can help your leaders feel like they are a part of something bigger than themselves and bigger than just their department. The frequency of the training is typically once or twice a year and can be offered year after year.

Now, let's break down each of these three phases of leadership development so that you can work to build them into your system. Ultimately you will choose one approach for Prepare, one for Equip, and one for Inspire to make up your Leadership Pipeline strategy.

Prepare New Leaders Using Experienced Leaders

The first step to move any potential leader up through the ranks of the Leadership Pipeline is by preparing them through strategic mentoring. This process will be critical at each juncture in the pipeline, not merely at the outset. Mentorship is the best way to ensure that any potential leader has the character and competency required to lead in their new role. Imagine the challenge of training leaders for a new role using a lecture approach alone. In this environment, it would be impossible to tell who was ready and equipped to step into a new position. Sure, someone might indicate that they desire to serve, but mentoring relationships are the only means of ensuring that they are ready to do so.

Jesus was a masterful mentor. Think about the passage in Matthew where Peter got a "sinking feeling" that he had just made a huge mistake. Notice how Jesus coached him in this situation: "But when he saw the wind, he was afraid and, beginning to sink, cried out, 'Lord, save me!' Immediately Jesus reached out his hand and caught him. 'You of little faith,' he said, 'why did you doubt?' And when they climbed into the boat, the wind died down" (Matthew 14:30–32).

My favorite part of the story is when Jesus walks over to Peter, who is halfway submerged under the water, and reaches out and takes him by the hand and asks a question in which He basically says, "Peter, let's talk." Jesus was capitalizing on a teachable moment. Instead of just rescuing Peter and putting him back in the boat, Jesus holds Peter's hand, keeps him afloat, and discusses what went wrong. Jesus looks at him and says, "Oh, you of little faith, why did you doubt?" I can imagine Peter's reaction.

Here he is, neck-deep in water, probably thinking, *Jesus, can we talk about this after we get back in the boat?* But Jesus wanted to talk about it right then, in the heat of the moment.

The question Jesus asked was very insightful: "You of little faith, why did you doubt?" The Greek word for *little* does not mean little in size, but little in duration. In other words, Jesus was saying, "Peter, your faith was big enough to step out of the boat and walk on water, but it wasn't the kind of faith that could endure the entire risk." What better time to learn that lesson than while literally neck-deep in trouble—I think Jesus had his undivided attention! Jesus was teaching him in the heat of the moment so he would never forget the lesson.

My greatest leadership learnings have taken place when I've had an experienced mentor by my side helping me debrief my experiences. The same is true for most new leaders, particularly those who are stepping into a leadership challenge or role they've never encountered. They are likely fearful and uncertain as to what the future holds and whether they have what it takes to lead at a new level.

Personal mentorship in the moment is the God-given means of calling out faith in leaders who are fearful they might sink. An experienced leader has been in this position before, so he or she has the relational capital to call the developing leader forward. Every developing leader needs a coach who will discuss, question, debrief, encourage, and challenge them at the appropriate times.

For this to happen, two things are necessary. First, we must have a team of current, experienced leaders who see it as a vital part of their job to mentor the next crop of leaders. This will not happen if existing leaders simply have their heads down and go about their ministry work alone. Leaders must look up and take responsibility for the leaders that are in the wings just waiting to be developed. Savvy leaders—particularly those over departments and entire organizations—must see it as a vital part of their ministry work to play matchmaker, pairing future leaders with existing leaders to aid in the development of these mentoring relationships.

Second, we must push beyond events to create a culture of life-on-life relationships and infuse daily tasks with intentionality so that future leaders are developed in an ongoing, organic way. If churches develop people only through events, relationships may or may not form, and these churches will passively train their people that leadership is best learned from an expert giving a presentation. But we all know that the best leadership lessons in life don't come through an event, they come when someone loves us enough to walk alongside us in the painstaking process of mentorship.

Mentorship is intimidating to many at first, but many lay leaders are willing to engage in the process. I was speaking to a group of leaders from a large church I was working with while taking them through the pipeline process. I closed my talk to the more than three hundred lay leaders by asking them to take out a three-by-five index card and select one of the following three options:

- I would be willing to identify new leaders.
- I would be willing to encourage existing leaders.
- I would be willing to mentor potential leaders.

I told them they could only select one option, or they could choose to not turn the card in, which meant they were unwilling to do any of the three. We received approximately 280 cards at the end of the night, and I divided the cards into stacks based on the responses. By far the largest stack, more than doubling any other stack, was the one indicating, "I would be willing to mentor potential leaders." The church staff were shocked.

I believe lay leaders are more than willing to step up and disciple others to lead at higher levels. But we must give them the chance. Often, the biggest thing standing in the way is a staff that is not giving them the opportunity to do so. We'll explore how this works in a later chapter.

As you think about preparing people to lead at new levels of leadership, there are three different approaches you can choose from.

Apprentice: Two to three potential leaders meeting with an existing leader anytime, any place, at any pace to review training modules that prepare them to lead in a particular ministry. Assignments are given in the context of the ministry environment where they can watch the experienced leader and then practice what they learn in the context of the real-time ministry environment.

Orientation: An established training schedule that takes place in a classroom-type setting with the focus of preparing three to five potential leaders to serve in an area of ministry. (Example: a group that meets every Sunday at 5:00 p.m. for six weeks.) Orientation class participants are matched with experienced leaders they can observe in real-time ministry situations.

Turbo Group: A group of three to five individuals meeting in a relational environment for short-term, hands-on experiential training with a goal of launching trainees into leadership. Learners are given scenarios to discuss and debrief how they would handle these situations. Where possible, they will also practice leadership skills with each other in the group. (Example: Potential worship leaders would be put in a turbo group together where they would rehearse leading, planning worship sets, and so forth. Potential small-group leaders would be put in a group together where they take turns leading and practicing the competencies of a small group leader.)

Put It into Practice

Take time with your team to discuss these three approaches to preparing new leaders and choose the one approach you can agree to use.

We will prepare people to lead at new levels through _____
(Apprentice, Orientation, or Turbo Group).

21

Equip Existing Leaders Using Peer-to-Peer Learning

When you have a leader for whom mentorship was a critical piece of his or her formation, but now he or she is in the rhythm of leading, what type of training would be the most effective next step in their leadership journey? The person who has been mentored is now empowered to lead without needing the same weekly, hands-on mentorship they received at the outset. It's likely—in fact it's preferable—that they graduate to a new form of training.

A great method for training that's frequently overlooked is peer-to-peer learning. This technique creates discussion among people who are at similar levels of experience, allowing them to learn from one another. Peer-to-peer learning has been shown to be one of the most effective means of sustained learning at any age level and especially in adults. In this method, peers are empowered to learn together while doing ministry.

Jesus and His disciples were making their way to Jerusalem when James and John asked if they could sit at Jesus' left and right when He came into His kingdom. When the others heard about this, they flipped out. Jesus responded by pulling the whole group together, engaging them in a discussion, and leveraging the experience to teach His team of disciples about servant leadership. I'm sure that emotions were running high and heated egos were on edge in the little circle of twelve. Jesus used this moment to teach His followers key lessons about the importance of servant leadership. He leveraged the conversation they had with one another to create a culture where genuine learning could take place (Mark 10).

There is a heightened receptivity to learning when people are facing problems. Why not huddle your leaders together and generate some discussion by allowing them to talk about the common leadership challenges they face in their role? This doesn't mean people need to only gripe about various facets of ministry. Leadership challenges, however, create a climate where authentic dialogue can take place and people can learn key lessons to avoid such problems in the future. People need a context where they can share what they are experiencing, discovering, and learning—about both themselves and leadership in the local church.

I'm convinced that one of the biggest missed leadership development opportunities today is collaborative learning. Many of us have heard the saying "all of us are smarter than one of us." However, very few churches structure leadership environments around this principle.

Those who truly want to see a culture of leadership development take root in their church should foster learning in medium-sized environments (five to twelve people) that prioritize peer-to-peer learning. There, a supervising leader can pull out the various tensions, challenges, and wins the group is experiencing and allow them to learn from one another. This means leaders of the organization will huddle with the leaders of departments, leaders of departments will huddle with the leaders of leaders in their area of ministry, and leaders of leaders will huddle with their leaders.

Coaching is a unique skill—one that will require a conscious shift for those who pride themselves in being expert teachers. For true peer-to-peer learning to take place, the expert must take a back seat and allow the overall group to move forward through shared learning. This doesn't mean that the coach loses his or her expertise, rather this person learns how to use it in a group so that the group collectively and collaboratively moves toward truth together.

The overall goal of this training is leadership development, but the specific training can vary based on the needs of the group or the problems they may be experiencing at any point in time. Ongoing team meetings, coaching huddles, or classes provide a valuable context to foster such peer-to-peer learning environments.

One time while doing a training with a church I asked the seven staff members how long they each had served in vocational ministry. When they tallied up their experience, they were shocked to learn that they had logged more than one hundred collective years of leadership. Then I looked at them and asked, "Do you think you can learn some things from each other?" The answer was obvious. Certainly they could learn from one another based on their shared background in local church ministry and the distinctive roles and contexts in which they had served. Their shared background provided a point of contact, whereby they all understood the unique pressures and victories that local church ministry produces. Their uniqueness provided diversity so that they could learn from the challenges, failures, and wins of those who had experienced things they may not have yet experienced. If this is true for the staff of a local church, how much more so for the various leadership teams in that church?

This is why I urge churches to get those leading in a particular ministry to huddle together to learn from one another's experiences. Imagine the powerful learning opportunity that exists when your student ministry small-group leaders huddle with a coach above them for some collaborative learning, or mission trip leaders meet with a coach above them to learn from their collective experience of leading teams of volunteers on overseas mission trips. Collectively these leaders have years of both positive and negative experiences they can share and learn from, sharpening one another's leadership competency.

As you think about equipping existing leaders, there are three different approaches you can choose from.

Huddles: Leaders at each level of the pipeline gather with the team directly under their leadership for a time of peer-to-peer learning. (For example, senior leaders of the organization would huddle with leaders of departments, leaders of departments would huddle with their leader of leaders, and their leader of leaders would huddle with the leaders that report to them.) Each ministry would ensure huddles are taking place on a regular basis in their area of ministry.

Classes: Leaders gather for occasional classes focused on leadership development. Classes can be ministry specific or general leadership. The class would include times for discussion where participants learn from each other's leadership experience.

Self-Directed: The church provides online training content that existing leaders can study on their own time for self-development. The training content would include videos or articles instructing them in key leadership competencies, assessments to help them evaluate their leadership, and assignments to help them grow in their skills. These leaders would be encouraged to discuss what they learn with their peers, but the church would schedule no formal gathering time. This is not a method that I recommend because generally I find if there is not accountability to discuss and apply the content, learning doesn't take place. However, there are some churches that use this approach. While it is not a recommended approach, it is better than not providing any ongoing development for your leaders.

Put It into Practice

Meet with your team and discuss which approach for providing ongoing development for your leaders would fit your church culture the best.

We will equip our existing leadership through _____ *(Huddles, Classes, or Self-Directed training).*

22

Inspire All Your Leaders Through Larger Gatherings

I confess I am a conference junkie. Catalyst, Leadership Summit, the ARC Conference—you name it, just give me more conferences. But why do I enjoy them so much? It's not the content; I can get that from a book, podcast, or YouTube. Conferences are beneficial for a variety of reasons, but for me one stands out—there's a unique energy when you're in a room with a crowd all learning the same thing. It's inspiring and energizing. That environment somehow creates a greater receptivity to new ideas, insights, and learning.

It seems that Jesus understood the power of conference experiences as well. Multiple times in the Gospels we see Him surrounded by thousands of people who had traveled long distances to hear Him teach. Check out Mark's report of what took place on one of these occasions.

> During those days another large crowd gathered. Since they had nothing to eat, Jesus called his disciples to him and said, "I have compassion for these people; they have already been with me three days and have nothing to eat. If I send them home hungry, they will collapse on the way, because some of them have come a long distance." (Mark 8:1–3)

The energy in those crowds must have been electric, because on two different occasions the people stayed to listen despite the fact they had run out of food. Jesus had to miraculously provide meals for the thousands who wanted to stay in that environment.

It's unlikely that many people are going to ignore their appetites to hear any of us present at a conference. Jesus certainly had a unique gift and a message that captivated those who listened to Him (and made others really, really mad). But large group venues do provide a certain buzz we should not ignore.

Don't miss the big point. If you fast-forward to large conferences simply because they are easier or more efficient, then you are set up to fail. Mentorship and peer-to-peer learning are a necessary precursor and support for the inspiration that comes from larger gatherings. You cannot choose one or the other. The system depends on each. That's why we've taken the time to tease out the unique facets of each in these chapters. Far too often, churches pick one method and use it as their approach for everything. And it doesn't work—at least not for long.

But, as the last step in a thoughtful system, large gatherings are a valuable tool. For one, they give us an opportunity to cast a unified vision to the entire group of current or future leaders. This is impossible to do in mentorship. Certainly, you hope that each mentor is effectively relaying the overall mission and vision of the church, but they can never communicate the exact same message to the exact same group of people in the same way that a leader can in a large conference venue.

Next, large venues give you a chance to share stories worthy of celebration. You should take advantage of this time and highlight those who have stepped into new leadership roles rather than merely using the same key leaders to do everything each time. By elevating new voices, you communicate to the group that leadership development is what we do. Following a time of celebration, you can use this setting to show appreciation for those who make the church's ministries function.

You can also leverage large groups to communicate fresh leadership insights, particularly those that you think are applicable to the wide range of leaders who are represented in the room. For example, this may be a great time to share about a new tool for onboarding future leaders that is going to be implemented throughout the church's departments.

Finally, and perhaps most importantly, large groups remind the various leaders that they are a part of something much bigger. It's easy to lead in a respective ministry and have little appreciation for the way that work plays into the larger mission of the church. When leaders sit in a room together, they can look around and see the various members of Christ's body working together as He intends. The relationships that form in such an environment may be key to motivating leaders to continue to persevere through the hard labor of loving and serving God's church.

Don't be afraid when we talk about large groups. Whether you are a church of fifty people, five hundred, or five thousand, you can utilize large groups to inspire leaders. For the church of fifty, this might mean thirty key leaders gathering in the church fellowship hall once or twice a year, whereas the church of five thousand may host an annual conference, book a national speaker, and invite area churches to participate. Whatever your size, you can make an investment in a large group event at least once a year. It is a small investment with a big payoff.

Many churches I've worked with have experienced this reality firsthand. The various ministries of the church each had their unique plan for developing leaders, so there was much overlap and duplication. As a result of implementing the Leadership Pipeline, they now have one centralized leadership development strategy—preparation sessions to train apprentices to move to the next level; huddles for ongoing equipping of existing leaders; and leadership gatherings where the leaders throughout the church gather for inspiration, information, networking, and training. The results have been contagious. For this to happen in your church, you will need effective content to use at each step of the process. This is the topic of the next section.

As you think about inspiring all your leaders, there are three different approaches you can choose from.

Conference: A gathering of all leadership churchwide one to two times a year for the purpose of inspirational development, vision casting, and celebration. These conferences generally last two to three hours. The agenda typically includes a main speaker followed by discussion groups where participants can talk about specific application to their leadership.

Rally: Each ministry area holds two to three rallies a year specifically for all those serving in their ministry. The agenda typically focuses on sharing the vision of that ministry, providing ministry-specific skills, and encouraging the team as a whole.

Workshop: A two- to three-hour training for leaders focused on general leadership development led by a field expert. Adult learning techniques such as group brainstorming, practice, and case studies are used to increase the interaction and learning of the participants. The focus is inspiring all leaders to grow and sharpen their leadership skills to impact the way they lead at home, work, and church.

Put It into Practice

Meet with your team and discuss which approach for providing inspirational training for your leaders would fit your church culture the best.

We will inspire all our leaders through _____
(Conference, Rally, or Workshop).

Prepare a chart as shown below, and fill in your approach to preparing, equipping, and inspiring your leaders.

Prepare	
Equip	
Inspire	

Now that you have decided the one approach you will take for the threefold approach to development, you can state the leadership development strategy of your church.

We will prepare new leaders through _____, *we will equip existing leaders through* _____, *and we will inspire all of our leaders through* _____.

Congratulations, you have now defined an intentional leadership development strategy for your church.

Part 5

Content

Create Training Content for the
Development of Leaders at Every
Level of the Leadership Pipeline

23

Information
Overload

In March 2010, I went with a group of friends to train pastors in Togo, Africa. Pastor Francis Avoy, who leads a ministry called Pioneers Togo, escorted us into various villages. One small village learned of the gospel only eight months before our arrival, and many had come to saving faith. Once known as the Village of Hell, this small community became known as the Village of Refuge after indigenous missionaries brought them the gospel.

Pastor Francis proudly introduced me to two men on his team he had been developing for some time: Pastor Yinka, responsible for leadership development, and Pastor Christophe, responsible for church planting. These two men had taken the gospel into that region and raised up a church planter named Silvus. Silvus was pastoring churches in a few villages in the region. As I was talking with Silvus about his work, he introduced me to Emanuel and Phillip, whom he was training and sending out to preach in other villages in the region.

As I stood in this village, I was moved by the power of leadership development. The discipling of leaders had not only impacted that little village but was now impacting the surrounding area with the gospel. While there, I was amazed to see how this team is taking the gospel to unreached people groups in remote villages, planting churches, and then raising up leaders in those villages to lead the church.

I was struck by the fact that this is just what they do. They were shocked that I was surprised at their level of multiplication of leaders. I was witnessing the power of four generations of multiplication. And that was commonplace for them. Why was this common for leaders in the Village of Hell, but so uncommon for most pastors and church leaders in North America? I see three problems.

Problem 1: Overdependence on Information

As I travel across the United States, I hear a common cry, "We don't have enough leaders." Which seems strange considering we live in a country where we are surrounded by leadership content. A Google search of the word *leadership* at the time of writing this chapter reveals more than 861 million results. If you search YouTube for the same topic, you get more than 20 million results. There are also more than 195,000 books on Amazon that address the topic of leadership. In other words, we are swimming in a rich pool of leadership content that can be used to develop leaders, yet leadership development seems to be one of the biggest problems in the church today.

Content is not the answer to this leadership development crisis. We don't need a new silver bullet to equip us with the content tracks on which our leadership development train can run. What we need is a relational, disciple-making process to equip our future leaders.

Problem 2: Unreproducible Process

There are many pastors and staff members who do develop leaders, but when you ask them to describe the process, they are unable to do so. They've done something intuitively that is impossible for others to reproduce. The multiplication process is hindered because, while they can add a few leaders here or there, no one else can reproduce what they've done. If you don't train someone how to develop a new leader in the process of developing them, then the whole reproduction process is in danger of coming to a halt.

Others create such complex systems, requiring such robust content, that only those who are exceptionally skilled and trained can reproduce their work. The vast amount of content can cause some to overengineer the process, making it more complex than it otherwise needs to be.

Either alternative—intuitive systems or complex systems—has the same outcome. They are not reproducible, thus their effectiveness is limited from the outset, even though the content that has been used in each case may have otherwise been solid.

Problem 3: Lack of Transformational Mind-set

I experienced the third problem in the area of content firsthand. In 1996, I felt called to plant a church and knew it was the scariest and riskiest thing I'd ever do in my life.

But there was no denying I was called to start a new church. I called my local denomination, and they invited me to a two-day church planter boot camp. I was passionate to learn, so I sat on the front row and gleaned every bit of wisdom I could about how to plant a new church.

My zeal quickly subsided when I sat and listened to an expert spend two eight-hour days filling in 273 blanks in his content guide. I'm certain the material had some beneficial elements, but this was lost on me. The boot camp was nothing more than a content dump, and I was crushed. I'm sure that the expert went home and told his wife, "Honey, I just trained twenty-five church planters!" But I went home and said, "Honey, I still don't know what I'm doing."

Most churches are using the same approach to develop leaders. They are putting twenty people in a room, lecturing to them for a few hours, and walking away feeling good about themselves because they've done leadership development. They may have, in fact, done more harm than good. You see, it's not leadership development if the leader isn't learning, growing, and changing.

While content is important, what is most important is that this content is used to produce transformation. We want leaders to be developed, which requires they grow and change. Information alone will not accomplish this goal.

Could you imagine registering to attend and get a degree from a university only to discover they have no curriculum or scope and sequence? You would withdraw immediately because you'd recognize the university is not structured with the tools they need to prepare you for a career. This is the same process many of our potential leaders experience when they come to us to equip and develop them to lead, only to find out that we have no clear plan in place and are simply figuring it out as we go along and hoping for the best.

I was talking with a discouraged group pastor one day. He was discouraged because he was struggling to get his leaders to attend his trainings. But when I began to diagnose the issues, it was evident he was strictly using an information-dump approach and his primary motivation was simply to make them better small-group leaders for his church. It didn't extend beyond that. Discipling of leaders can be so much more. I've discovered that people value what adds value to them. If our leadership development adds value to their lives as a parent, spouse, community leader, and a leader in the marketplace and the church, they will value it much more. They will lean into the process of transformation because they see the fruit in all of life.

For example, Joe Haddad, a lay leader at Cuyahoga Valley Church, said, "The Leadership Greenhouse (pipeline) reminds me that we are leaders in the body of Christ—the church leadership of church members is not just the responsibility of the pastors on staff. As a LifeGroup leader, the church is entrusting me to be a coach, shepherd, anchor, blueprint, and scout. I can only do that through the Holy Spirit. . . . The concepts I've learned throughout this Greenhouse training are transferable to my role as a leader in my company."

This is what we are after!

24

Evaluating Change

To produce transformation, we've got to begin by asking "How?" How does change really happen? I think there are three elements—a triad of development—that produce the type of transformation we long to see.

KNOWLEDGE

COACHING　　　　**EXPERIENCE**

First is *knowledge*. If I want to have a great golf swing, I go out and buy *Golf Magazine* and read an article on the five steps of the perfect golf swing. This knowledge is important, but it's unlikely to change my golf swing if that information is all I have. I need another element—*experience*. So, I grab my nine iron and go in the backyard and swing one thousand times. All the while, I'm doing the best I can to apply the knowledge I've read to the swing I'm practicing. Does that transform my golf swing? Maybe. Maybe not. In fact, if I am doing something wrong in my swing during practice, I may be reinforcing bad habits rather than a good swing. Many of the leaders in our church are leading week in and week out without anyone observing them, encouraging them, or giving them feedback. As a result they may be developing some bad leadership habits that keep them from being as effective as they could be. But when a third element is added in, transformation is possible. I also need *coaching*. I know the form for a proper swing, I'm practicing in my backyard, and now I invite my buddy who is a golf coach over to watch and give me feedback. Now transformation takes place.

When you embrace this triad of development, you will begin to see real change in those you lead. As I mentioned before, it's not leadership development unless the beliefs and behaviors of our leaders are changing. The triad of development will ensure transformation in your leaders.

Several years ago, my middle son, Jordan, got a job at a popular restaurant chain. He came home after a week raving about the training. When I asked him what he liked about it, he explained how every day he would have to eat a different appetizer, meal, and dessert because that was how they were training him to memorize the menu. He also watched a video on serving and discussed it with his trainer. Finally, he described how the bartender sat down with the new servers and taught them techniques for getting 20 percent tips. He was thrilled, and he became a great server.

Brianna, my daughter, got a job at the local pizza place the same week. But her experience was very different. Her first day on the job, she walked it at 11:30 and the manager told her he had to leave to run errands. She would be on her own as the sole server and checkout clerk. She explained to him it was her first day and she didn't know the menu or how to use the register. He told her, "You can figure it out, but ask the chef if you need some help." And he left. She quit after about a week because she felt so incompetent.

My son's boss wanted him to learn specific skills to do the job well. My daughter's boss threw her in without explaining what success looked like or training her for the work. As we saw earlier, it will take knowledge, experience, and coaching to train leaders effectively. Each of these components were used in my son's training, which is what made it such a positive experience.

What might this look like in the church? How do we prepare new leaders to lead, and what content should we use to prepare them? It's important that we begin to put this together using the overall flow we're developing in this book. We can't merely jump to content without having an effective culture, structure, or system in place. After you define and align your structure, onboarding, and training system, then we can turn our attention to the content that would best fit that pipeline.

When I am working with a church, I ask them to draw their Leadership Pipeline structure on a giant Post-it and then write in the content they are using to develop leaders at each level. I make clear that I am not talking about job descriptions, policy manuals, or any other documentation like that. Rather, we are looking for content that equips their new leaders in the competencies they need to lead at various levels.

As you might imagine, that exercise doesn't take very long. Very few churches use specific content to train new leaders at any of the levels of the Leadership Pipeline. Once they have their pictures drawn, we put them all together and discuss four questions:

- What is working?
- What's missing?

- What's confusing?
- What needs to be changed?

It's easy for churches to get discouraged or overwhelmed at this point. Realizing you have no content available to equip your new leaders can be disheartening. But recognizing the problem is the first step to solving it. It might help to pause for a moment and go to www.maclakeonline.com and download the Content IS worksheet to determine the current reality of the content you use to develop leaders.

Take a mental inventory of your leadership development pipeline and consider what content you use at each step. Then, ask yourself the four questions above. What did you learn about the process?

Most pastors lack a clear plan. In the face of an abundance of content, they lack the ability to pull content together in a coherent way that properly combines knowledge, experience, and coaching. In this section I want to walk you through the process of putting together the leadership competencies for each level of your Leadership Pipeline. Then I will show you how you can put together content for that training using the "prepare, equip, inspire" paradigm we developed in the previous section.

25

Choose Your Leadership
Competencies

Several years ago a children's pastor asked me to meet him for lunch to talk through the challenges he was having with leadership development. After we sat down, I told him we needed to reverse engineer his process so we could identify the location of the problem. I asked him to explain how he was developing his leaders.

He told me that he would find four or five new leaders and ask them to follow him around on a Sunday morning as he showed them various roles within the children's ministry. After two weeks of shadowing, he would plug these new leaders into roles that seemed to fit them best. This leader captured a helpful facet of leadership development. Shadowing is a valuable way for most to learn a new skill. I was still stumped as to the problem.

He explained that he would place them in the roles only to find that they weren't very good at the role or weren't doing what was expected. Because he lacked a mechanism for training, these new leaders would grow discouraged and give up. After a month or two, they'd drop out.

I asked what competencies they needed for these roles and how the shadowing process was used to instill this knowledge. At this point, the children's pastor had no answer. To make my point, I took out a pen and began to tap out the rhythm to a song on the table. I asked him to identify the song. He couldn't. I tried again. Even though it was a very familiar song, he was at a loss. I continued a few more times, and my friend could never name the song. I finally told him I was tapping "Amazing Grace"—a song I was certain he'd heard hundreds of times. I asked, "Why didn't you know that song?" He answered, "Because it was in your head and not mine."

The point was clear. This was exactly what he was doing with his leaders. He knew the rhythms of children's ministry and what it would take for them to be successful. He understood the essential competencies that were necessary. He assumed that others could quickly catch on. It seemed so simple to him—like the rhythm to "Amazing Grace" was to me—but they could not figure it out. If he wanted to truly train leaders, he was going to have to take what was in his head and get it out and into the heads of others.

Paul instructed Timothy, "What you heard from me, keep as the *pattern* of sound teaching" (2 Timothy 1:13, emphasis mine). The Greek word for *pattern* is a word that was used to speak of a builder who would lay the framework of a house before he would build the house. He would lay out a pattern and then build on it. Future leaders need patterns if they are going to step up into new levels of responsibility. These patterns should be specific competencies we want our leaders to learn. There are several benefits that come when you create shared competencies.

Shared Expectations

First, spelling out specific competencies we want our leaders to learn helps them understand what is expected of them. They know what success looks like from the very beginning rather than being surprised when they get in and struggle to keep up. They know how we expect them to lead. Without this level of clarity, a new leader may make assumptions or default to old or bad leadership habits.

I heard a conference speaker tell a story about a senior pastor who was dissatisfied with the leadership performance of his student pastor.

He called him into his office to fire him. Because he was nervous about firing him, he just started talking to him and asking questions. The more he asked, the more he learned about what the young man was doing. He discovered that the young man was visiting the high school and middle schools each week. He also learned that he had built a student leadership team that was planning their Wednesday night service. He was surprised to hear of this work, so instead of firing him he gave him a raise.

The senior pastor had expectations for his student pastor, but because these expectations were unstated, he was frustrated because he assumed the young man wasn't doing what he wanted. It's likely true that the student pastor was frustrated with the senior pastor as well. I've learned that if we don't have shared expectations with our leaders, we will have shared frustrations. Sharing the specific leadership competencies for each level will create a sense of shared expectations that will help your new leaders get off to a good start.

Greater Confidence

Next, if leaders understand the competencies we expect, then they will likely have greater confidence in their roles. All people doubt themselves when they are unsure they are hitting the mark. But if they see clearly what is expected, they can know they are meeting, or exceeding, what they are being asked to do.

I've never taken a job or a volunteer role where the organization told me, "Mac, thanks for being on the team, here are five essential competencies you will need to demonstrate to really be effective at this role. And we are going to equip you in these competencies." Imagine the difference it would make in our leaders' level of confidence if we told them about and trained them in the competencies we expect right up front.

Helpful Coaching

When my friend Brian Bloye and I started a church planting network called Launch, one of the first things we did was interview dozens of church planters and ask them what it was about their leadership that made them effective planters. After a few months of this, a pattern emerged. I took all our notes and identified twelve leadership competencies for church planters that we turned into the Multiply Church Planter Training curriculum. Our trainers would spend six months training a small group of three to five new church planters in these twelve leadership competencies.

Years later, I could spin back to these same planters and discuss any challenges they were facing using the same twelve competencies. I could ask them to identify their core issue based on which of the twelve competencies was being challenged in their present situation. I've found that pointing people back to the competencies is a powerful tool for leadership coaching. The same is true in local church leadership. If people know what they need to know and be able to do, then we can help coach them to success.

In 2011 Tanner Turley, a young, gifted pastor, moved his family just outside Boston to Medford, Massachusetts, to plant Redemption Hill Church.

Boston is not an easy city for planting a church or recruiting new church leaders. People are skeptical of the gospel and resistant to outsiders. Despite these challenges God blessed Redemption Hill's efforts, and they began to reach people and grow the church. As the church was growing, they identified leaders and did their best to equip them. They felt they were growing their leaders' character and giving them a good theological understanding but weren't helping their leaders grow in the skills they needed to lead well. Tanner said they "were not reproducing quality leaders fast enough in our growing church and transient context (with leaders moving out of the city). This meant our pastors were directing too many ministries and not free to focus in our greatest areas of gifting/strength."[1] Tanner understood that leadership skills were a necessary corollary to robust theological training.

After going through the Leadership Pipeline training, he and his team put together their Leadership Pipeline structure and the competencies that go with each level. They immediately began to implement this training. Here are Redemption Hill's Leadership Pipeline competencies:

LEADERSHIP PIPELINE

A holistic roadmap for leaders to develop leaders in the character and competencies of Christ.

SENIOR LEADERSHIP - Leads the Church

Provides visionary leadership for the church as a whole by:
- Inspiring and equipping to vision
- Strategic planning (corporate)
- Managing the pipeline
- Organizational execution
- Persevering past barriers

DIRECTOR - Leads a Ministry

Provides visionary leadership to execute an overall ministry by:
- Strategic planning (ministry)
- Stewarding a budget
- Leading meetings
- Improving systems
- Decision-making

COACH - Leads Leaders

Encourages and guides a group of leaders within a ministry by:
- 1 to 1 meetings
- Encouraging leaders
- Providing evaluation
- Situational leadership
- Solving problems

LEADER - Leads Others

Provides leadership for a small team or group by:
- Mobilizing people
- Caring for people
- Delegating responsibility
- Carefronting in love

PARTICIPANT - Leads Self

Participates in a group or team as a growing disciple by:
- Learning the Word
- Following Jesus
- Loving the church
- Serving others
- Sharing the gospel
- Multiplying disciples

And eight months later they had people leading at levels they never had before. He and his team equipped three volunteers to lead at the director level and eight new people to lead at the coach level. Identifying these competencies gave them a framework by which they could disciple leaders to greater levels of responsibility. Tanner said,

> We recognized we needed to equip our leaders with specific skills to help them lead in the heat of the moment but did not have a road map. Identifying competencies for each level of the pipeline brought incredible focus and freedom! By identifying nonnegotiable skills, we have focused our energy in training and given our leaders confidence for their respective roles. Most importantly, these competencies are catalyzing greater ministry effectiveness, which means people are growing in grace with greater efficiency.[2]

This is the fruit of clear competencies for the various stages of the pipeline, which then empowers the church to create training modules to move people through their defined process.

Now that you understand the importance of identifying competencies at the various levels of your pipeline, spend some time with your team discussing what competencies you think are essential at each level. Keep in mind that the competencies at the leader level may be different based on the different ministries, but the competencies at the leader of leaders level and the rest of the way up your Leadership Pipeline will likely be the same regardless of the ministry.

Below is a sample of what it might look like. Once you have completed your competency list, think of it as a discipleship pathway for the leaders and potential leaders in your church.

SAMPLE COMPETENCY LIST

GROUPS

1. Facilitate discussion in a way that everyone engages
2. Deal with difficult people in a way that honors the individual and the group
3. Mobilize my group to serve the needs of others
4. Build a sense of biblical community among my group members
5. Identify and develop emerging leaders

MISSIONS

1. Understand and motivate different personality types
2. Build a sense of biblical community among my group members
3. Deal with difficult people in a way that honors the individual and the group
4. Help others to adapt to and connect with people of different cultures
5. Identify and develop emerging leaders

WORSHIP

1. Model and lead worship in an engaging way from the stage
2. Build thematic worship sets that flow and lead people to encounter God
3. Communicate and coordinate with the band members
4. Handle mistakes, failures, and criticism in a way that honors God and others
5. Lead a productive postservice evaluation with your team

STUDENTS

1. Facilitate discussion in a way that each student engages
2. Deal with difficult participants in a way that honors the individual and the group
3. Understand and motivate different personality types
4. Connect with students in a way that builds trust and relationship
5. Identify and develop emerging leaders

CHILDREN

1. Facilitate discussion in a way that each child engages
2. Deal with difficult students in a way that honors the individual and the group
3. Connect with students in a way that builds trust and relationship
4. Relate to parents in a way that provides a sense of confidence and security
5. Identify and develop emerging leaders

COACHES COMPETENCIES

1. Lead an encouraging and challenging one-on-one meeting with a leader
2. Lead an engaging huddle that sharpens the leadership competencies of your leaders
3. Provide feedback and evaluation that increases ministry effectiveness and leadership confidence
4. Encourage leaders in a way that shapes their souls
5. Make decisions that guard the mission and values of the church

DIRECTOR COMPETENCIES

1. Build and steward a healthy ministry budget
2. Manage and coach team members toward priority goals
3. Lead meetings that bring about results
4. Cast a vision that motivates and mobilizes your team
5. Hire, fire, and reposition talent

SENIOR LEADERSHIP

1. Guide and guard organizational DNA
2. Manage the Leadership Pipeline
3. Capture and cast future vision
4. Execute organizational plans
5. Persevere through difficultly to get to the next level

26

Write Prepare Modules

Early in my ministry career, like many other young leaders I was struggling with learning how to lead. That's when I stumbled upon John Maxwell's *Developing the Leader Within You*. His book was transformational for me. It was a practical guide for a young leader that taught me how to have influence, solve problems, cast vision, navigate change, and more! I loved it.

So when I planted Carolina Forest Community Church in 1997, I wanted some of my leaders to discover what I had learned from Maxwell. I began to take some of them through the book chapter by chapter. Those were some of my first efforts in discipling leaders.

They loved the book, too, and I saw it impact their lives and leadership. I leveraged this content to develop leaders in my context, and it worked. Unfortunately, many pastors hand their staff or key leaders books and articles and ask them to read the content in isolation. They then wonder why the content fails to produce the transformation they desire. Far too often we gather leaders at the church and regurgitate information to passive spectators who listen to the experts talk.

First, this method of utilizing content fails to capitalize on a person's internal motivation to learn. We tend to make excuses for people and say they won't do any homework; therefore, we wait for them to show up so we can give them the instruction. We need to give people more credit for being motivated to learn on their own. In our technological world, people are learning new information constantly, at the touch of a screen. Modern leaders can leverage these tools to train their leaders and empower them to learn on their own.

Second, this method assumes leaders can only be developed when they are with us. To increase our leadership development impact, we must provide potential leaders with resources that stimulate their learning even when they are away from the "teacher." Too often our concept of training is limited to "classroom time" or time when the learner is with a mentor. I've learned that I can multiply my influence and take advantage of training leaders when they are away from me as well.

Jesus couldn't give His disciples a book or a CD, so He taught them using parables. These short, memorable stories were filled with tension or paradox and caused them to go away and think about what He was teaching. In fact, Mark 4:33–34 says, "With many similar parables Jesus spoke the word to them, as much as they could understand. He did not say anything to them without using a parable. But when he was alone with his own disciples, he explained everything." Jesus' intent was to get His followers to think for themselves and wrestle with the principles He was teaching. Then later He would discuss and explain it to them.

This is the best method for preparing future leaders. Remember back in the systems section, we discussed the prepare stage. It's during this time that we are equipping future leaders to move up to the next level of leadership. We can train them by deploying content they can study in their discretionary time that teaches the essential competencies we need them to learn. Here's how we create training modules that prepare future leaders.

Step 1—Find Potential Content That Already Exists

This first step should give you hope. Far too often, leaders crumble under the weight of developing new content to train future leaders. It takes a lot of time and mental energy to do this well. Why not capitalize on great content that a respected leader has already created?

As I mentioned earlier, there is great leadership content available today through the internet, podcasts, books, blogs, and more. Instead of creating your own content, invest some time finding great content that already exists. You probably already know of trusted voices that speak to issues that matter to your leaders. Whether it is theological foundations or practical application, there is content out there you can use. Once you've developed a list of competencies you're looking for at each stage in the process, you can find strategic content that speaks to these practical skills.

Step 2—Put an Assignment with Each Competency

Identify the content—whether an article, book chapter, or podcast—then build specific assignments that force future leaders to experience and practice the specific competency.

To do this you want to consider two things as you write assignments. First, think of assignments that will help them practice the competency in the context of the ministry position. Keep in mind they are not in the new leadership position yet. So they will practice the competencies under the mentorship of an existing leader. Second, design assignments so they can practice the competency at home and work. Remember we want to help them not just turn our ministry widget but equip them to live a biblical lifestyle of leadership.

Step 3—Write Questions to Help Them Process What They're Learning

Questions are crucial. These are what will help the new leader process the content and integrate it into their thinking and behaviors. The men and women doing the training can leverage these questions as an ideal guide for coaching.

Attempt to develop questions around Scripture, content, and assignments. Take each area and develop a few good questions to help the developing leader process what they are learning. Sadly, many leaders don't know how to ask good questions, so here are a few pointers.

- Ask open-ended questions.
- Ask questions that are not easy or obvious but are appropriately challenging.
- Ask questions that reflect on their previous experiences.
- Ask questions that force self-assessment.

Here are some solid examples of good questions:

- What traits of spiritual leadership have you admired in one of your previous small-group leaders/pastor/boss?
- What are common mistakes small-group leaders make when asking questions?

Years ago, I grew frustrated that I was reading a lot but not retaining as much as I'd like. I wrote the following eight questions to help myself get more out of what I was reading or listening to.

1. What challenged you the most?
2. What questions did this raise for you?
3. What leadership strengths did this affirm in you?
4. What growth areas did this reveal for you?
5. What scripture teaches or illustrates the concepts from this content?
6. What is one way you can put this into practice before you meet to discuss this with your trainer?

7. What are three to five action steps you need to take?
8. What accountability question would you like for me to ask you next time we meet?

Here's the key to building your content quickly. Take these eight questions and put them with a podcast, blog post, or chapter of a book, and you have a ready-made training module. For examples of prepare modules, go to www.multiplicationeffect.com/content, and you will find downloadable content you can use to help train your leaders.

Step 4—Evaluate, Modify, and Make It Better

Three years after I wrote the Multiply Church Planter Training material, I had taken six different groups of planters through the training. I was in my office one day looking at a pile of notes I had taken during three years of doing this training. It hit me that I had learned a lot after doing the training six different semesters. So I began to go back through it and evaluate and add insights and ideas I had gleaned along the way. This made the content significantly better than when it originally came out.

I recommend churches build their content, start using it, and get feedback so they can make improvements to their original content. By getting user feedback, you'll discover what works and what doesn't work.

These simple training modules are designed to prepare future leaders. Once they are in place, you are ready to put together content to equip already existing leaders, which is the subject of the next chapter.

27

Provide Ongoing Equip Training

Now that you've effectively developed prepare modules, you are ready to take the next step in training leaders. Remember, this step is just as vital as the work you do to prepare a leader to take the next step up in the Leadership Pipeline. It would be easy to assume that your work is over once your new leader is in place, but if you neglect the ongoing equipping of existing leaders, you are setting them up for potential frustration or limiting their impact from a lack of growing as a leader.

A big part of leading a team is gathering for a time of mutual encouragement and shared learning. Equip trainings are not about the leader teaching the team but facilitating discussion in a way that peer-to-peer learning takes place. Regardless if you choose to use Huddles or the Class approach, this training functions best when you follow the six-part agenda that follows. Obviously if you chose to use the Self-Directed approach there is no formal meeting to plan for.

Connect

Spend the first ten minutes as everyone arrives allowing the leaders to connect. Have snacks or drinks available and music playing as everyone enters the room. Start with a prompt like: "Share a highlight

149

from your time with your family over the past month," or "What is your favorite coffee shop in town and why?"

The purpose of this question is just to get the leaders mingling and to foster connection with one another. Since some of these leaders may have been serving for a while, it is likely that a few will already know one another. But some may not. And you can rest assured that everyone comes to a huddle in a bit of a blur, based on the pace of life for most. It's good to provide time for the leaders to take a deep breath and talk in an informal way before you segue into content geared more specifically for training.

Celebrate

One of the most important things you can do when leading a huddle is to lead your team in celebrating recent wins. Spend five minutes asking your team to share something they've seen God do in their area of ministry since the last time you gathered. This might be the successful completion of an event that blessed the community, the integration of new leaders on the team, or the fruit of life change in the people your team serves. As each person shares, use this as an opportunity to reinforce important values or leadership lessons that naturally emerge from the moment. Though this time is not overtly oriented to training, you can use these moments of celebration to remind the group of the reasons behind what they're doing.

Check Up

Spend a few minutes asking everyone how they applied what they learned from the previous training. This will refresh their memories and reinforce what they are learning. The implications of leadership development are not the kind that produce change quickly (at least not in most cases). It will take some time for leaders to embody the ideas you are trying to instill through these huddles. This check-up time gives them the space and margin to admit they are still in process and developing as leaders.

You don't have to spend a lot of time on this, but a simple checkup on how they've applied what they've been learning will help them stay mindful to continue to practice what they've been learning.

Coach

The coaching segment usually lasts thirty to forty minutes. If you use the Huddle approach, the entire coaching time is a guided discussion around a specific leadership topic. The idea is to get the leaders learning from one another's wisdom and experience. Here is an example of what a huddle might look like.

This is an opportunity for your team to discuss what they have learned from their experiences regarding leading with intentionality. Introduce the topic of leading with intentionality with a personal illustration, then have someone read Mark 1:32–39. After reading the passage, discuss the following questions.

- How would you describe Jesus' pace of life?
- What phrases in this passage give hints to Jesus' intentionality?
- We see Jesus being pressured by others. What tends to pull you away from leading with intentionality?
- How do you choose what not to do?
- What is your greatest burden for those you lead in this area?

Close the coaching time by taking five minutes to summarize some key leadership lessons from this passage. Here are a few suggested principles you might highlight.

1. Intentionality in our private lives leads to intentionality in our leadership.
2. When I lead with intentionality, I will disappoint people.
3. Intentionality means saying no to good things so you can say yes to the best things.
4. Intentionality requires clearly defining your objectives.
5. Intentionality takes discipline and focus.

That's it. Nothing flashy or time intensive. Go to my website www.maclakeonline.com and download free samples of huddles. You should be able to pull this portion together with just a bit of time and intentionality. And, since most of the leaders in the room have been serving for some time, there will be plenty of wisdom to go around. Plus, since they are serving together, there is a level of credibility and respect they will give to one another that they might not even give to a singular teacher up front.

When I am on-site training a church in this part of the leadership development process, I frequently model how simple a huddle can be. I will gather a small team of seven to ten people around me and ask a question to introduce the leadership topic. Next, I read a passage or show a short three- to five-minute leadership video. Then I simply ask how the content applies to their leadership. As I lead the discussion, I try to draw off their experience and expertise rather than inserting my own. Each time I model this, there is great enthusiasm in the room about how easy but effective these types of huddles can be for existing leaders.

If you chose the Class approach to equipping existing leaders it doesn't look much different. Instead of facilitating discussion the whole time you may start by having someone do a ten- to fifteen-minute TED talk–type of teaching. Or you could show a fifteen-minute leadership video you found on Youtube. After the teaching portion you open it up to the leaders to share their insights and allow for a time of collaborative learning.

Care

Use the next ten minutes to have your team members share personal prayer requests and have them pray for one another. There are a couple of things to watch for here. First, don't skip or rush through this time. If you do, you will passively communicate that prayer is an arbitrary add-on rather than a core discipline. Second, challenge the group to stay personal in their requests. Rather than sharing needs and concerns about those they lead, push the group to talk about the challenges or issues each is facing as a leader.

Communicate

Finally, close the time by sharing important announcements that affect everyone in the room. This may be letting them know about an important event coming up in your area of ministry or an important churchwide event that is coming up. Make sure you also let them know of the time, date, and location of the next equip training session.

These six steps—connect, celebrate, check up, coach, care, and communicate—serve as the flow for an effective training. And they're at play in all effective organizations. At one point in my life I worked in real estate. Every Thursday our broker would pull us together for a huddle. In these conversations we'd celebrate wins and hone ongoing skills we could never learn in real estate school. Or, recently I was in Target and noticed the red shirt brigade circled up behind a register. The manager was reading a letter from a customer that praised the customer service of his team. He used this win to praise his group and to push them to excel still more. Churches can, and should, utilize huddles in the same way if they hope to see leaders thrive in their roles. For more samples of equip trainings go to my website www.multiplicationeffect.com/content.

Inspire with Great Training for All

The final aspect of the leadership development strategy is designed to inspire leaders through motivational training experiences. Unlike the first two training environments, these events will be infrequent and are designed for a large group. The intent is to get all the church's leaders together to provide a leadership training event that is high quality and inspiring.

The first time I did a large group training to inspire leaders was in 1994 when I hosted an event for the leaders at Pawleys Island Baptist Church. We gathered on Sunday night once a month, where we would eat and do an interactive training on very practical leadership topics such as vision casting, delegation, dealing with conflict, soul care, or how to lead a meeting. Though I now think monthly meetings like this are too frequent, we still experienced great fruit from these types of training.

The Sunday night event was designed solely for our leaders. Because the quality was high, we had others asking to attend, but we intentionally restricted the attendance to just those who were leading in our church. We always had at least 90 percent of our leaders there, and they would leave telling us not only how they were applying these principles in their church roles but also how these training events were affecting their work in the marketplace. A principal of a local school told me how she was taking notes and teaching the concepts to her teachers. A real estate broker repeated the lesson with his sales agents. It was exciting because the training wasn't just teaching them to lead in ministry but was equipping them to live a biblical lifestyle of leadership. They valued the training because it added value to them as leaders at home, work, and ministry.

While the huddles were informal environments designed for peer-to-peer learning, the Inspire trainings are built for large groups and designed to motivate. The large group meant that more planning was required to make them happen. When doing Inspire trainings it may require renting a venue other than the church or coordinating additional details, such as childcare, to make it easier for your leaders to participate. The goal of motivation and inspiration means that more time will be needed to go into planning the content that would be presented. You will need to think through not only the content itself but the way you would present that content to make sure it touches the hearts and minds of those in attendance.

One of the churches that I've worked with on Leadership Pipeline is Hope Church in Las Vegas, Nevada. They call their biannual inspire event *Leadership LIVE*. Using *LIVE* as an acrostic, in every single inspire event, they desire to *listen, intercede,* cast *vision,* and *equip.*

Listen: This portion of the inspire event is devoted to hearing from their leaders (questionnaires, surveys, etc.). They might take time during the event itself to collect this data or have some strategic way of gathering content before or after the event.

Intercede: This portion of the inspire event is devoted to praying together for God's activity in Las Vegas, the western United States, and the world. Again, it's important that this not be a mere transitional element during the conference, but that strategic, intentional time is spent interceding for the work God is doing in their midst.

Vision: This portion of the inspire event is devoted to communicating high-level vision. Often the senior pastor or another key leader uses this time to remind the church of God's mission and present some clearly articulated sense of where God is leading them in the future.

Equip: This portion of the inspire event is devoted to teaching general leadership principles that can be applied to any area of life and ministry. The conference leaders invest energy to ensure that clear, definable action steps are spelled out in such a way that all those in attendance know their next steps.

Hope Church recently hosted this inspire event for their leaders and cast vision for the next ten to fifteen years of God's activity in and through their church. This allowed senior leadership to lay out key, strategic next steps for their church. Because the conference was designed for core leaders, the church was able to motivate these key stakeholders and call them to elevate their own personal involvement and investment in God's activity in Las Vegas, the West, and the world. The event rallied leaders together around the mission of God being accomplished through them. It brought a sense of excitement and energy to their leaders, knowing where God is taking them as a church and that it involves them, the core leadership of Hope Church.

In fact, during the event, they gave their leaders an opportunity to share what they felt was exciting, encouraging, or challenging about the vision that they heard. That gave the senior leadership team an avenue for real-time feedback to monitor if any changes needed to be made when casting vision for the church as a whole in the future. For Hope Church, the value of this type of environment allowed for strategic communication of vision to their core leadership first and a place to gain the feedback to modify their vision language if needed.

Regardless of which approach you take to provide inspire training for your leaders (Conference, Rally, or Seminar), make sure it is done well and they leave challenged and motivated to use their gifts and strengths to make a kingdom impact.

Part 6

People

Identify, Equip, and Empower
Leaders to Develop Leaders

A Centralized Approach
to Developing Leaders

29

Who is developing leaders in your church or organization? Most people answer that question by saying, "No one" or "That would be Joe's job."

Here's the problem: when leadership development isn't clearly defined and assigned, it never happens. If only one person is responsible for leadership development, then we can rest assured that there will never be enough new leaders to accomplish the mission we're after. There's no way you can have an exponential multiplication of new leaders if you have bottlenecked the process by using only one person.

This reality hit me in 2007. I was asked to oversee the leadership development classes at Seacoast Church. I observed classes like this before and knew I didn't want to do the traditional sixty-minute lecture approach. So that year I wrote and taught the classes using adult learning techniques. We only had about twenty people in attendance each week, but they seemed to genuinely love the process. I, on the other hand, was discouraged, because I could not single-handedly develop enough leaders. As the year ended I began to evaluate the impact and effectiveness of this approach.

That's when I identified six challenges to the normative program-oriented approach to leadership development.

The Challenge of Busyness

We held the classes on Wednesday nights at seven o'clock for eight consecutive weeks during a semester. Few people were able to make all the classes. Most already had something planned that would keep them away for at least one week, and others had unexpected things come up that meant they missed a week here or there. Their children would have a ballgame, they would have to stay over at work to finish an important project, or a family member would have a birthday party or become ill.

I'll never forget when I was in Bible college, I was sick the day my professor taught how to do a funeral in my Pastoral Duties class. Five years later I was in a panic when I was asked to do a funeral because I didn't have a clue. And I wasn't about to tell them I couldn't do it because I missed the "How to Do a Funeral" class. When we depend strictly on a classroom approach to prepare new leaders, we take a risk that they will miss essential training sessions and thus have a gap in their development.

The Challenge of Timing

The classes had defined start and end dates. We might start a leadership class in the second week of September and run through the middle of November. It was inevitable that someone would come up to me in the middle of that semester and express interest in becoming a leader. The only thing I knew to tell them was to wait until the next semester when they could get started from the beginning. I lost a lot of good volunteer leaders that way. By the time the next semester training rolled around, they had lost interest or found another area in which to serve.

The Challenge of Distance

Many churches will reach people within a reasonable driving distance to the church facility. But there are those highly committed people who will drive a longer distance to be involved in your church. Many times, those who drive the farthest are some of the best, highly motivated leaders you might have. But because they live so far away from the church, the distance makes it difficult for them to drive all the way back in the middle of the week for leader training.

The Challenge of Relational Loyalty

As we would finish a semester of training new leaders, I would assign these men and women to a pastor on our staff. I was surprised when many of these newly trained leaders came to me and requested to serve under my leadership. That's when I would inform them that wasn't what I did; I simply trained leaders and they would now need to learn to serve under another pastor. Many wanted to continue serving with me because I had just spent two months getting to know them, training them, believing in them, helping them discover their strengths, giving them feedback, and helping them grow as leaders. When you invest in the gifts and talents of a new leader, there is a relational loyalty that is built between you and that leader. There is a special bond that is hard to replicate in new relationships.

The Challenge of an Artificial Learning Environment

I loved using adult learning techniques because it didn't just give learners important information—it forced them to think and discover truths on their own. Often, I would force leaders to engage their peers in discussion or provide coaching feedback during the training itself so they were practicing what they were learning. But there was one big problem—each learner would only get one practice rep in front of the group and it would be limited by time. I remember telling new small-group leaders in their practice round that there would be fifteen minutes for them to lead in discussion. It didn't matter how good it was, or how much the Holy Spirit was moving in that moment, when the alarm went off, your time was up. We would then evaluate and let the next person lead for fifteen minutes. While this was a helpful practice, it was still an artificial learning environment that made true learning difficult.

Think about it: When we want to train someone to swim, where do we train them? A swimming pool. But when we train small-group leaders how to facilitate discussion and build a sense of community among a small group, where do we do that? Typically, a lecture-based classroom. Many of our training environments never give the learners an opportunity in the real world to practice the skills we are teaching them.

The Challenge of Self-Selected Leadership

Most churches I've been involved with growing up used the same leadership recruitment method. The pastor would announce from the stage that we need new leaders and would ask people to sign up on a sign-up sheet in the back of the auditorium. Those who signed up would be invited to a leadership training class, and these new recruits would be the new crop of leaders.

That was my default mode as well. I would make sure there was an announcement made that new leadership classes were starting up, and we would invite anyone and everyone to attend. The challenge with this approach is that many high-capacity leaders don't respond to these types of calls. And the flip side of this challenge is that some people sign up whose next step is definitely not leadership. Some of those who would sign up for our leadership class where still struggling to lead themselves.

These are the six challenges of what I call a program-oriented approach to leadership development. And sometimes we know these problems exist, but we don't change the way we do leadership development. We just keep doing the same thing, just trying harder and failing to get the results we want. There has to be a better way of developing leaders. That's why I made a big shift from a program-oriented approach to a people-oriented approach to leadership development.

With a people-oriented approach you decentralize leadership development. Leadership development begins to take on a form that looks more like discipleship the way Jesus did it. And when you take this approach, sudden busyness, timing, distance, relational loyalty, artificial learning environments, and self-selected leadership are no longer barriers. By releasing leaders to develop leaders, coaches to develop coaches, and directors to develop directors, you've empowered your leadership to prepare and equip leaders any time, any place, at any pace, and eliminated the challenges of a typical program-oriented approach.

30

Evaluate the Health
of Your Pipeline

While pastoring Carolina Forest Community Church, I was the volunteer chaplain for the local high school football team. Every Friday during football season I would be on the sidelines dressed in coach's garb, getting an up-close and personal view of the game.

During one particular game that was going badly for us, I saw our coach pacing the sidelines looking at a laminated paper. As he grew more agitated, he threw the paper in the air and it landed on the field as he walked away. I ran out on the field and grabbed the paper. Once back on the sidelines, I looked and saw it was the team depth chart. I had never seen one, so I was fascinated. The front page was titled "Offense," and it had all eleven positions and the names of the players who could play each position. The flip side was titled "Defense," and again it had all eleven positions with the names of those who could play each of those positions.

When I saw this, the first thought that hit me was, *Why don't I have a depth chart for my church?* I rolled up the paper, stuck it in my pocket, and took it to my staff meeting Monday morning. I handed out copies to each of my staff and apologized. I told them I was sorry I wasn't leading them well. Here, a high school football coach knew every position and every player on his team, yet I couldn't identify the leaders in each of our ministries. I didn't know who had the potential to move into various leadership roles. I told them we led the most

167

important mission on earth and yet I had failed to have a good picture of the team that would help us accomplish that mission.

I asked them to put together a team picture and turn it in to me by the end of the week. From that point on, we began to track who was on the team, who was leading, and who had the potential to move into leadership roles in the future. And it's been a practice I've maintained since that day.

The mission of the church is significant, and it requires people to move it forward. You can have a huge vision, but if you don't have people on your team, the vision will not become a reality. The more and better leaders we have, the more likely we are to move the needle of our vision.

When it comes to the people portion of the Leadership Pipeline, there are several things we must evaluate to move to a more people-oriented approach to development.

Who Are the Leaders We Have?

It has been my experience that many leadership teams cannot tell you how many leaders they have. We would all agree that the greatest asset you have is your people, yet many leaders can't tell you who is leading where within their church. They may have a vague notion that many are serving, but they can't name the leaders who are carrying key weight in the church's mission. You cannot maximize the talent in your church until you know who is on your team.

How Many Leaders Do We Need?

Knowing who is on your team is important, but you also need to know how many additional leaders you need. If your church were to grow by

15 percent, how would that impact your need for leaders? It's wise to know that number ahead of time so you can be proactively developing leaders rather than reactively trying to fill positions.

Do We Have Good Leadership Ratios?

You will remember back in chapter 13 you determined healthy ratios for your area of ministry. But sometimes as the church grows your ratios can become too large. Ratios are important because they can determine the health of the relationship between a leader and the team. Ratios are calculated by dividing the number of leaders by the number of team members. This needs to be done at each level of your Leadership Pipeline so you can identify if you have healthy or unhealthy ratios. Ratios can vary by ministry, but a general healthy ratio of leader of organization to leader of a department is one to five, and leader of a department to leader of leaders is typically one to ten. A leader of leaders to leader of others is one to five, and leader to team member varies widely based on the different ministry. A leader of a grade-school classroom may be one to seven, while a leader of an adult small group might be as many as one to sixteen. Personally, I like smaller ratios because communication, collaboration, and connecting is much easier.

Who Has the Potential to Move to the Next Level?

How intentional are you at looking at future talent in your church? Typically, churches look for new leaders in August and January when we're about to ramp up a new season of ministry. But looking at our potential leadership pool needs to be a regular discipline if we hope to build a culture of leadership development.

How Many Developers Do We Have?

One of the common measures churches use in their standard metrics is how many small groups they have. That's an important number—as in many cases the small-group leaders are the ones we depend on to disciple those attending our church. But there's another key metric we should look at more closely. How many leaders are producing new leaders? If we know how many are helping us disciple people, we should also know how many are helping us disciple new leaders.

Jeff Moody, pastor of Revolve Church, took his team through the Leadership Pipeline training when his church was five years old. The team knew how to reach people, and they were experiencing growth and seeing people baptized. The team eagerly took what they learned and began to apply it. This process has dramatically impacted his leaders' ability to equip new leaders. For the first time they have a pool of leaders who are trained and ready. In fact, they have more leaders than positions, so they are using the newly equipped leaders as coleaders for existing teams. God has blessed the church and they've grown by 25 percent in the last year, and because his leaders learned how to develop leaders, they were ready to receive this growth.

Put It into Practice

So now it's your turn. Go to www.multiplicationeffect.com/people and download the worksheet to help you build out your team picture for your area of ministry.

31

A People-Oriented
Approach

One morning I was struggling with the program-oriented approach to leadership development. It was too restrictive. There were just so many barriers, as we mentioned in a previous chapter. How can a church ever develop enough quality leaders using this approach? The question haunted me.

That morning I was doing my devotions through Ephesians 4 and that changed everything. I read the words, "So Christ himself gave the apostles, the prophets, the evangelists, the pastors and teachers, to equip his people for works of service, so that the body of Christ may be built up" (Ephesians 4:11–12). The Holy Spirit caused me to pause on these two verses. As I reread these words, I thought I understood my job as a professional pastor was to develop leaders. Again, the Spirit prompted me to take a closer look. That's when it hit me. The apostles, prophets, evangelists, pastors, and teachers were not professional church staff. They weren't paid staff. That morning I wrote down my paraphrase of Ephesians 4:11–12: *He has given leaders to equip the saints to do the work of ministry.*

That means that the entire Leadership Pipeline is charged with the mission of developing leaders. My imagination went wild as I asked the question, what if? What if we took Ephesians 4:11–12 seriously and began to decentralize leadership development? What might change about the leadership landscape of the church if we empowered leaders to disciple new leaders? That vision has not left me to this day.

This is what I began to call the people-oriented approach to leadership development. And the advantages are huge.

The Advantage of Time

You no longer must wait for a new semester of classes to start in order to train new leaders. When you have leaders ready and released to train new leaders, you can start any time. All you need are relationships. When God has moved on someone's heart to take the step into leadership, they shouldn't have to wait, and in a people-centered approach to development, they no longer have to.

The Advantage of Place

Typically, leadership development has been done at the church building. But with the people-oriented approach, you can train leaders anywhere. No more having to drive long distances back to the church to be trained. Leaders can meet with those they are training at a coffee shop, restaurant, or even in their own homes. Even better, leaders can be trained in the context of their ministry work.

The Advantage of Pace

With the traditional program-oriented approach, leadership training is held on a specific day and time each week. If you miss, well, too bad. But with the people-oriented approach you can meet at a pace that fits the leader. When I first started doing this approach to development, I had a guy who worked for IBM and frequently traveled overseas. I identified him and one other man in my group to train as new small-group leaders. After going over one of the training modules at a local restaurant, we would schedule our next session. Because he had a crazy schedule, we were able to create a pace of training that worked for him. He never missed a session because it was easy to schedule a time for the three of us to connect to review what they were learning.

The Advantage of Relational Loyalty

When a single staff member is the one doing all the training, those who are trained will always look to that individual for ongoing development or help with leadership challenges. But in the people-oriented approach, new trainees learn to look to those lay leaders who discipled them through the leadership training. This relational loyalty will aid in shared ministry work in the years that follow.

The Advantage of Real-Life Experience

In the program-oriented approach to developing leaders, trainees rarely get the opportunity to practice the skills they're learning. But in the people-oriented approach, potential leaders are walking alongside an existing leader, observing them in action. In this context they are also given the opportunity to practice the skills they are learning. This allows the trainer to give them feedback and help them further develop their leadership competencies.

The Advantage of Leader-Selected Leaders

With the program-oriented approach, churches typically make an announcement about leadership training and anyone can show up. But in the people-oriented approach, you empower your existing leaders to look in the context of their ministry and identify people who have the potential to lead and invite them into the training.

Please understand that programs don't develop leaders, leaders develop leaders. Leaders ask me all the time what the best program, book, or curriculum is for developing leaders. We're always looking for a magic bullet. The magic bullet is *you*. I can train a great leader with a bad curriculum, because leaders develop leaders.

People develop people. Think about what grew you the most as a leader. It was most likely another leader. Leadership is caught as much as it is taught. Leadership development is most effective when it's done in the context of relationship.

32

Building Your Farm
Team System

Branch Rickey was an innovative leader in Major League Baseball who understood the power of leadership development to the future success of any organization. Elected to the Baseball Hall of Fame in 1967, Rickey is best known for signing the first African American player to take the field in the big leagues. Yet his true greatness came through the introduction of the modern farm system.

At the time, major league teams often simply purchased the players they wanted from prominent minor league clubs. Rickey grew frustrated, however, when players he scouted in the minor leagues went to wealthier rivals in the pros. As general manager of the St. Louis Cardinals, Rickey devised a better option. He convinced the Cardinals ownership to purchase and control minor league teams ranging from Class D players up to the highest minor league level, Class AA. Since the Cardinals now controlled an entire minor league farm system, they could promote and demote players as they chose to grow their own talent over time. Using this model, the Cardinals developed enough talent to enable them to win nine National League pennants and six World Series championships between 1926 and 1946. It wasn't long until other major league teams saw the power of this system and started following suit.

Your Leadership Pipeline is your church's farm system. The Leadership Pipeline you define becomes a progressive way to give people greater opportunities to develop in the context of the local church and then move them to greater levels of leadership in the future. You have all the human resources you need to build a winning team, but you must leverage those people to create a farm system that will work—and continue to work—over time.

In many ways the first disciples were the original farm system for the church. They certainly would not have understood themselves in this way when Jesus first called them (Matthew 4:19). This original call of Jesus was infused with leadership development. They would be developed by Jesus, and He, in turn, would use them to develop others.

Jesus took hold of these ordinary men and did extraordinary things through them because He had a high confidence in their potential. And these first followers were not exactly the types of people who had leadership potential just oozing out of them. They were a mismatched assortment of obscure men who were made great by God's power. He had confidence that He could, and would, build the church on the strength of these leaders.

Churches need to have the same confidence in those God sends their way. He is continuing the work of building His church, and He is doing so by sending the exact right mix of gifts and abilities to local churches to continue the mission He has given His body. We should have confidence in those we have because we have confidence in the God we serve.

Unfortunately, we often lack confidence in the people we have or undermine their confidence in themselves through our failure to develop them fully. We see them doing something wrong, and rather than coaching them up, we shake our heads and walk away—all the while secretly thinking that there is no way we are ever going to get anything done with this type of ineffective leader.

Here's an equation I have found to work over and over again. *The greater the confidence I put in those I mentor and lead, the greater confidence they will have in themselves.* The greater the confidence they have in themselves, the greater likelihood they will reach their God-given potential. If they reach their God-given potential, then we will effectively fulfill God's plans and purposes for our local church.

One of the exercises I do with churches is to have each ministry department list all those who are serving at each level of their pipeline on one giant Post-it. I ask them to look at the names and put an up arrow beside any of those who they feel may have the potential to move up to the next level of the Leadership Pipeline. After giving them about fifteen minutes to process, we come back and the group shares their observations. Every time I lead this exercise, one of the observations they share is that they saw the potential of people they had never noticed previously. So often there can be dormant leadership potential in our members that we are overlooking. The Leadership Pipeline helps you look with fresh eyes at who may have the potential to move to another level of leadership.

Sean Sears planted Grace Church in Boston. The church struggled to grow the first four years, unable to break one hundred in attendance. Sean was suddenly connected with a high-capacity pastor from Dallas who began to coach him monthly. At the same time, he and a small team of people went through the Leadership Pipeline training I was doing in Atlanta. Sean, one of the best leaders I've come across, suddenly had the coaching plus a system to develop leaders.

It wasn't long before the church began to grow and reach people. They had to first build out a plan for developing leaders, and then God sent a huge growth curve to the church. When Grace needed a new children's director, they looked at the names in their Leadership Pipeline. Looking among their coaches in the various ministries, they identified Gail. Gail had been developed as a coach in the first impressions ministry and had been leading well there. They knew Gail understood and fit their culture, so it was a natural move to transition her into a new role. They took her through the ministry director competencies and onboarded Gail as their new children's director. Gail left her full-time job and now serves full-time on Grace Church staff. This is the fruit of a system to develop leaders. Today the Grace Church Leadership Pipeline is so robust and they have such a constant flow of potential church planters in their church that they are sending out to plant more churches all across Boston.

Put It into Practice

Now it's your turn. Go to www.multiplicationeffect.com and download a sample of this exercise. In an earlier chapter you created your team picture by inserting the names of all those serving in your area of ministry on your Leadership Pipeline. Now take that same chart and put an up arrow by those you think may have the calling and potential to develop the competencies to lead at the next level.

What surprised you when you looked at your list?

What encouraged you?

What next steps do you need to take with those who have the potential to move to the next level of your Leadership Pipeline?

33

Choose Key People
as Trainers

I'm always looking to learn more about leadership development from anyone I can. So one day I approached the manager at my local Starbucks and asked if he would meet with me to share how Starbucks develops leaders. This twenty-eight-year-old enthusiastically agreed, so we set up a time to meet the following week.

That morning I showed up an hour early and grabbed a seat at one of the long tables that seats eight people. To my surprise, five minutes after sitting down, three women in green aprons sat at the other end of the table. It didn't take me long to see that one of these women was doing a training session with two new baristas. I had come to learn how Starbucks developed their people and was getting a front-row seat to watch it happen one hour before the manager was to meet with me.

I sat and listened to this trainer ask great questions, share her experiences, and debrief the video they had watched before their session. She asked questions about what they had observed as they had shadowed her. It was about a forty-five-minute training session during which these new employees were learning essential competencies to do their jobs well.

A little later the manager came over to my table, where I had fifteen questions scripted to learn all about Starbucks's approach to leadership development. This young man pulled out a training manual and, as I asked questions, pointed me to the manual, showing me the

Leadership Pipeline levels with essential competencies and training modules used to develop leaders at each level. He didn't hesitate when I asked what would happen if he wanted to move up in the organization. He turned to the page showing competencies of a regional manager and told me how a current RM would begin to work with him to develop him to that level.

The leaders at Starbucks are empowered to develop other leaders, and they know it. There is a hidden power in this that we often overlook. Leaders who develop leaders become better leaders.

I discovered this when I wrote the Multiply Church Planter Training curriculum. After writing the training I was a little nervous about how it would work. So I gave it the first test drive. That first six-month semester I trained four new church planters. At the end of the training, I knew some things could be improved, but I was pleased with the general flow. Immediately I jumped into the second semester, kicking off my second cohort of three planters. Once again, I saw the training worked well, but I began to notice a related benefit I had not expected. As a trainer, I was learning as I was working through each of the twelve competencies I had written. After leading my third cohort I was excited to lead it again and again because I discovered that each time I taught the twelve competencies I grew myself and became a better leader as a result.

Imagine what would happen if you empowered some of your leaders at each level to develop new leaders up to their level. The small-group leader who trains two or three new group leaders in the context of his group, using the five competency modules you put together, is now going to get better and better himself each time he trains new leaders! Imagine the impact it would have if you could empower your coaches with the responsibility of developing new coaches. Not only will it make them better coaches, it will free up your time to lead at a higher level.

The immediate response I get when I share this with church leaders is reluctance—they just don't think they could get their leaders to do that. Here's the good news. You don't have to get all your leaders to be trainers. You only need 20 percent to get the flywheel started. Once this smaller percentage begins to develop and train future leaders, you'll have a small army of people who will recruit others to become trainers in due time.

Many times when I talk to pastors about renewing their leadership development efforts, their first instinct is to ask their leaders to choose an apprentice. I quickly warn them not to take this route. That always surprises them a little bit. *You mean to tell me the guy who is here to teach us leadership development doesn't want all our leaders to have an apprentice?*

While it sounds like a good approach, apprenticeship may hurt your leadership development efforts. I typically poll attendees at a training I'm conducting and ask them what percentage of their current leaders would find and train an apprentice if asked. I've never heard a number higher than 30 percent. If we are experiencing a 70 percent failure rate, there is no way we will ever build a culture of leadership development.

I was coaching a pastor through leadership development a few years ago when he came to me in a panic. He told me the new church semester was coming up and he didn't have enough small-group leaders. I took the opportunity to ask him a series of questions to get the basic information and help him process his leadership shortage crisis. His church was running around 300 people. He had 150 in small groups and had 15 group leaders. His church was growing by 15 percent. Once I drew this information out from him, I told him I would show him how simple math would ease his anxiety and solve his problem. I showed him that if his church was growing by 15 percent, he would have 345 people in attendance twelve months from now.

Based on his current percentage, he would have about 175 in groups. But let's say you aren't happy with that. Let's bump that up to

190. That means he would need 19 group leaders. He has 15, but let's assume he will lose 2 of those. That means he needs a total of 6 new leaders. This is where the power of 20 percent comes in. Let's take 20 percent of your existing leaders and identify them as trainers of new leaders.

That would give us three leaders who would continue to lead their group, but we would ask them to use the prepare training modules to equip two to three new leaders. If we did this with three of your existing leaders, that would give us a total of six to nine new leaders by the end of the year. Here's the power of 20 percent: you only need 20 percent of your existing leaders developing new leaders to keep pace with a 15 percent growth rate.

But 100 percent of those at the leading departments level and up should always be developing leaders. Remember back in section 1, when we talked about building a culture of leadership development, we said one of the keys to building a culture is expecting your key leaders to be reproducing new leaders. If someone is leading at the department level, then one of your key expectations is they are constantly developing leaders.

Our end goal is to produce an abundant harvest of reproducing leaders. When we look not just at the leaders we need, but we identify, equip, and empower existing leaders to disciple new leaders, we will begin to see our Leadership Pipelines being filled with a constant flow of leaders at every level. Leveraging a few quality trainers, we could create a magnificent family tree of leaders akin to what you see in coaching football circles. A coaching tree describes the way current coaches were trained and developed from a common master teacher. For example, Bill Walsh led the San Francisco 49ers to three Super Bowl Championships during his remarkable career. Along the way, he trained and developed coaches like Tony Dungy, Mike Holmgren, Mike McCarthy, Lovie Smith, Mike Shanahan, Mike Tomlin, and Jon Gruden. Coach Walsh's tree would have accounted for twenty-eight of the thirty-two head coaches in the NFL during the 2013 season. This is what would happen if we had a few key leaders with this type of family tree of leadership development among the people God sends to our churches.

Put It into Practice

Now once again, it's your turn. Go back and review the names of those you put on your team picture. But this time identify those who could be potential trainers at each level of your pipeline. Go to www.multiplicationeffect.com/people and download a sample of this exercise.

Part 7

Outcome

Deploy Your Plan in the Context
of Real Relationships

34

Now It's Go Time

You may find yourself feeling a bit overwhelmed at this point. We've now built a Leadership Pipeline that is culturally appropriate for your local church. Now it's time to deploy this plan in the context of real-life relationships. There are two temptations to fight against at this point.

The first is being *crippled by fear of failure or insecurity* about your ability. In my early years of ministry, a young man approached me and asked if I would mentor him in leadership. I was flattered and shocked at the request. I quickly agreed, mostly because it fed my ego more than the fact that I saw great leadership potential in this person.

I set up our first meeting at a local coffee shop, and I spent an hour asking him about his life story and the areas in which he wanted to grow. The first meeting could not have gone better. Our second meeting, two weeks later, also went well as he shared his sense of his strengths and gifts and discussed the abilities he brought to the leadership conversation. After that meeting I went home feeling good about what we had done but feeling confused about what was next because I had shared everything I knew about leadership in our first two meetings. What was I going to do now?

When he called to schedule another meeting, I found an excuse not to meet. To be honest, it wasn't that I was busy, I just didn't know how to structure my time with him. Sadly, I continued to put him off until he finally stopped calling. I had failed big time in my first attempt at leadership development because I was afraid to simply keep meeting and continue the conversation.

It breaks my heart today when I see church leaders struggle to produce leaders because of fear. Most of the time it's not from lack of desire but from lack of know-how and a fear of failure. This doesn't have to be the case. I've worked hard throughout this book to make the process of leadership development accessible to all types of leaders. Whether you exude confidence or shirk back, you now have the tools you need to develop leaders well. Any neglect on your part is a work of Satan attempting to divert you from prioritizing the things that truly matter.

The second temptation is *feeling like you must do everything immediately*. In fact, that's the worst thing you can do. Announcing this Leadership Pipeline like it's the next big program in the church is the surest way to ensure that it will not work. The design is meant to be people-oriented, not program-oriented, so don't sabotage your plan by bypassing people and running to a program. Don't roll this out big and bold. Start small, on the grassroots level with just a few key leaders and future leaders. Get some wins in the rearview mirror working with a small group, and, in time, you can rest assured that it will pick up momentum.

I met with Pastor Muriithi Wanjau of Mavuno Church located in Nairobi, Kenya. Mavuno Church, which was started in 2005, has had a rich heritage in their few short years of discipleship and making leaders. A multisite church boasting ten locations, they created a discipleship program called Rooted that garnered international fame, and they have a leadership residency that is cranking out leaders. In other words, Pastor Muriithi knows a thing or two about multiplication.

I was speaking to a large group on leadership development when Pastor Muriithi approached me during a break. We found out we both had been impacted in a big way by Ram Charan's work in *The*

Leadership Pipeline. We struck up a lively and energizing conversation about leadership development. That's when he said something I will never forget. In his rich African accent, he said, "Mac, it takes four generations of reproduction to build a culture of leadership development."

I've shared that wisdom again and again, because here in the United States, we want leadership development to be fast, easy, and linear, but it's not. It takes time. It's slow, messy, and customized to the needs of the learner. When we try to do leadership development quickly, we rob people of the full opportunity to develop their skills under the watchful eye of an experienced leader. We never see Jesus rushing anyone's development. *We* make the mistake of valuing fast results. But one of the most important characteristics of a leadership developer is patience.

Confident patience.

Patient confidence.

That's what we are running after when we begin putting it all together by implementing our Leadership Pipeline. Rest in God's work in—and through—your efforts to learn and embody the principles of this book, and trust that He will produce the fruit in His time and in His way.

A friend of mine told a devastating story about his house. He said that he and his wife recognized there was some sort of problem with their home. He then contacted a specialist only to discover the bad news that there were structural issues with the foundation. He asked his friend how much it was going to cost to repair the foundation. He was astonished when he was given the estimate of $18,000. He asked what would happen if they decided not to fix the foundation. The specialist told him that they would be fine for a couple of years, but the foundation would continue to get worse and eventually they would not be able to sell the home. And, worse, over time the house would eventually begin to implode. Knowing that he didn't have a choice, he paid the contractor and fixed the foundation of his home. He told me they finished the work on August 1 of that year, but he said that someone who drove by the home in July and again in August would have noticed no difference, though they'd invested thousands of dollars in the home.

Building a culture of leadership development in your church organization is a lot of work. You must pay the high price of putting in the time and exerting the effort to help your team shift paradigms from doing to developing. That's not an easy job. However, if you make this investment, it will impact the long-term health and vitality of your church. It will not make the lights in your auditorium any brighter or the sound any better, nor will it attract more unchurched people to your church or make your guests feel at ease. But the investment will strengthen the foundation of leadership and make your church stronger and healthier for the long term. While it is a large investment, it's not an investment you can afford to ignore.

There's a principle I always share each time I lead a church through building the Leadership Pipeline. You must choose your pain. Inevitably, halfway through the process, some of the staff begin to grumble about the amount of work and how difficult it is. At this point, maintaining the life of a "doer" looks pretty attractive. That's when I always tell them it's at this point you get to choose your pain. You can choose the pain of having a shortage of leaders and doing all the work yourself. Or you can choose the pain of building an intentional and reproducible leadership system that will fill your Leadership Pipeline and expand the leadership load out into the hands of others. The choice is yours, and now is the time to make it.

35

Designing with the
End in Mind

What kind of leader do you want to develop? Not what kind do you want to find, but what kind do you want to develop? My guess is you want leaders who

- are men and women of character,
- embody the values of your organization,
- inspire others to follow,
- think biblically and decide wisely,
- give their all to the cause,
- display patience and perseverance, and
- are committed to reproducing themselves in other leaders.

Leaders like this aren't built in the classroom—they're built on the battlefield of the mission. Leaders like this aren't built from reading a book—they're built from the challenge of putting content into action. Leaders like this aren't built by just jumping in and figuring it out—they're built through constant input and feedback from an experienced leader. Leaders like this aren't built in a day—they're built over a season.

One of my favorite verses related to leadership development is Acts 4:13: "When they saw the courage of Peter and John and realized that they were unschooled, ordinary men, they were astonished and they took note that these men had been with Jesus." Jesus' three years of intense discipleship with these men had come to an end. They were out expanding the mission like never before. Jesus told them that He's prepared them for great works, even greater works than He's accomplished in His earthly ministry. Now was that time. It's in this season we really begin to see the leadership impact Jesus had on these men.

These were not men who were trained to follow a policy and procedures manual, nor were they just turning the ministry widgets to make sure the ministry machine kept running smoothly. No, these were men who were displaying courage they had learned under Jesus as they deeply engaged spiritual warfare. They were men who were expressing an unmatched faith as they reached out their hands to heal the broken. They were men who reflected back to their first mission assignment from Jesus when He sent them out two by two telling them to "pray to the Lord of the harvest to bring forth workers" (Luke 10:2, paraphrase). These were men who were bent on taking new territory for the kingdom of heaven.

This type of mission-fueled, Spirit-filled passion is the outcome of our leadership development efforts. It's worth whatever cost we must pay along the way to see people live into God's good purposes for their lives. It's a mission compelling enough to motivate our daily agendas and shape our priorities around the mission of leadership development.

As one who has read this book, you are now positioned to bring change to your church in the area of leadership development. Whether you are a senior leader or a staff member, you can take steps to embody the ideas we've discussed. And, it's incumbent on you to do just that. When you take your eyes off leadership development it ceases to become a priority in the culture of your organization. If you, as a leader, don't keep it front and center, then no one else will. I would go so far to say no one else can.

It's your voice above any other that shapes the values of the organization. What you value you talk about, and you measure and build accountability systems to ensure results. Thus it stands to reason if you're not talking about leadership development on a regular basis, then that value loses power and dies or at best becomes an aspirational value.

Leadership development requires discipline, discussion, and accountability if it's going to thrive. The urgent will always have a greater pull than what is truly important. That's why you must keep development in the forefront of the minds of your leaders.

Here are six questions you should ask your department leaders on a regular basis. And as a bonus, I will include some follow-up questions for each one.

1. *Who are you developing?*
Follow-Ups: Who could step in and do what you do if you were unexpectedly unable to do your role? What parts of your role are you giving away or sharing on a regular basis?

2. *How many leaders do you have at each level of your pipeline?*
Follow-Ups: How many do you need? How would you describe the health of your Leadership Pipeline? How has your leadership bench deepened over the past four months? Which level of your pipeline is the strongest? Weakest?

3. *Who are the new potential leaders who are coming up in your area?*
Follow-Ups: Which of your leaders is mentoring them? To what level are these potential leaders being developed? Which ones are you most excited about? Why?

4. *How many of the leaders in your area are currently reproducing themselves?*
Follow-Ups: What are you doing to help them in these efforts? What are you doing to celebrate the reproduction of new leaders in your area?

5. *What is the biggest obstacle you face in seeing a continual repro-duction of leaders in your department?*

Follow-Ups: What resources or support do you need to help you do this more effectively? How can I help?

6. *What are you doing currently to grow yourself?*

Follow-Ups: What character or competency do you need to focus on developing over the next few months? How can I help?

It is your discipline of keeping leadership development front and center that will discipline your leaders to keep it front and center. In time, with intentionality on your part, you will see the type of change that will produce the leaders you dream of having.

Keith Cowart, former lead pastor of Christ Community Church in Columbus, Georgia, listed leadership development as one of the key responsibilities of his role as senior pastor. Before going through the Leadership Pipeline process, Keith already had a strong incli-nation toward developing leaders. Keith planted CCC in 1997 and over the years pastored this healthy, growing church that impacts the community. His church implemented the Leadership Pipeline process and is seeing an abundant harvest of fruit as a result. Derrick is one example.

Derrick came to the church as a successful Realtor. He shared with Keith that he felt a nagging sense that he had been neglecting a calling on his life. Keith began to work with Derrick to get him involved in leadership—first as a volunteer with the outreach minis-try of the church. Before long, Derrick was leading this ministry of more than four hundred people. Derrick soon moved from quarter-time to part-time and eventually to full-time executive pastor at CCC. The church used the principles of the Leadership Pipeline to coach him along the way and into each new role. Six years later Keith announced to his church that he was handing the baton of leadership to Derrick, and in fall 2018 Derrick became the lead pastor at CCC. Keith moved on to provide regional leadership for his denomination. This is the type of fruit that comes from a local church-based Leadership Pipeline.

36

Multiplying Multipliers

One of the primary goals of leadership development is not just to produce a leader but to produce a leader who produces leaders. *Developing a leader will last a season, but developing a leader who reproduces leaders lasts generations.*

Several years ago, a young man walked into my office and with great enthusiasm in his voice said, "Mac, if you know anyone who needs Jesus, please give me their name because I love to witness, and I just want to share my faith all I can." Knowing this guy had the gift of evangelism and was leading people to Christ regularly, I said, "Tim, do you want to live a life of addition or multiplication?"

He paused, thought, and said, "Multiplication, of course, but what are you getting at?" I said, "You have an amazing gift for evangelism and you can keep winning people to Christ one at a time, living a life of addition, or you can live a life of multiplication by equipping others to share their faith." Then, looking him in the eye, I said, "Tim, I want to challenge you to train one hundred people in our church how to share their faith." This was like pouring fuel on a fire—he was now a man on a mission and said, "Yes! That is what I want to do."

Within six months he had trained dozens of people how to share their faith. He never made it to the one hundred goal because during that six months God called him into ministry and he left to attend seminary. I still hear from him on occasion and he is still equipping people to share their faith; in fact he has trained many more than one hundred throughout the years.

God's impact through our lives will reach its maximum influence when we focus on multiplying multipliers.

In 2010 I was hired by Pastor Brian Bloye at West Ridge Church in Atlanta to start a church-planting network called Launch. Brian and I, along with a small team of people, dreamed about the possibilities of training church planters in a way that focused on developing them in their leadership. In our first year, not only did we build the unique assessment process but we also created a transformational training process to take church planters through before they started at their churches. We had a dream of church planters being trained in small cohorts by trained facilitators in the context in which they would be planting. Our ambitious goal was to see church planters assessed and trained in context by people from that location.

This meant that our church plant training events would not be held in a major city, taught by one or two experts a couple of times a year. Instead it would be taught in small cohorts wherever planters were at work. This would require us to have hundreds of trained facilitators across North America. So we created a reproducible process for training trainers. This approach to empowering local trainers to develop church planters in relational small groups was having a big impact, so much so that it caught the attention of the North American Mission Board (NAMB), the church-planting arm of the Southern Baptist Convention. Eventually we partnered with NAMB, giving them this training approach. At the time of this writing there are more than four hundred church plant trainers across North America. Each of these trainers is using the content we developed and seeing measurable results in health and effectiveness. And what excites me is that because there is a development system in place, this number will continue to grow exponentially.

I love the role God allowed me to play in this journey because on a regular basis I get emails or Facebook messages from church planters and trainers whom I've never met thanking me for the training that was provided. This training curriculum, along with the small cohort approach, gave us a plan and a process for seeing a huge multiplication effect of planters who are training planters. Here's the big lesson I've learned from this experience: when you make leadership development intentional, then you can make it reproducible, and when it is reproducible, it becomes unstoppable.

When you give your team an intentional leadership development strategy that is aligned across all your ministries, you're giving them a gift. You will see their level of confidence grow as developers, as you execute the strategy over and over again.

I have a driving passion to see believers at all levels of the Leadership Pipeline reproducing themselves in potential leaders. And hopefully through this book you have seen that it's not that difficult to see a multiplication effect in your church or your ministry department. Leadership development is simply building a relationship with someone you believe in and helping them take their next step as a spiritual leader. It's not a class you take. It's an intentional relationship you build.

One of my favorite Leadership Pipeline experiences came when I was leading a large group of church staff through this process. As I mentioned earlier, one of the things I do while on-site is take them through a model prepare session. I had sent the training module two weeks in advance and told everyone to read the content, do the exercises, and be prepared to discuss what they learned. (Note the Triad of Development in action.) There were more than seventy people in the room that doubled as a worship center and gym. I explained to this large crowd that I would not be training all of them in this module but instead I would choose three people to join me around a table while everyone else observed from the bleachers.

The seventy's assignment was to watch intently and write down observations about what they learned from this relational, transformational approach to training. For sixty minutes I guided my three "trainees" through the prepare module as the crowd watched. I asked questions, drew insights from their experience, challenged them with thoughtful follow-up questions, pointed out strengths I saw in them, and helped them assess their current ability related to the competency we were discussing.

When the time was up, I turned to the crowd and asked for their observations. They enthusiastically shared their insights. Then one lady stood up, pointed to the small table where I did the training, and exclaimed, "I can do that!" Next she pointed to the stage and said, "I cannot do that."

Like this young lady, so many people view leadership development as being a lecture-oriented experience. They simply see it as an expert standing on the stage delivering everything they know about leadership for those who are sitting ready to learn. If they are not good at outlining a talk, or an eloquent speaker, they disqualify themselves as a leader developer.

This is why I do that model experience. I want people to see that leadership development doesn't have to be that hard. It's building a relationship, believing in people's potential, and guiding them through a series of intentional discussions that prepares them to lead at a new level. We are simply discipling people to lead like Jesus.

Remember that as a teenager I had a burning passion to make a difference for Christ. But I was told repeatedly I was not a leader. I was shy, awkward, and lacked confidence. I probably would've just settled for a life, as important as it is, as a doer. But God saw fit to put a man in my life who discipled me in leadership and transformed the way I saw myself. And because of that I gained the courage to pour myself into discipling more leaders. Today I look back over my shoulder and I see an army of men and women God has placed in my life. People I'm proud of. People I've invested in. People who are now picking up the mantle and reproducing themselves in the lives of others. When Jesus said, "Go make disciples," He meant teaching them to live like Him as well as lead like Him. This is something we can all do.

Even me!

Notes

CHAPTER 5: MISSING A MARK WE'VE NEVER DEFINED
1. LifeWay Research, "CRD Training Project" (Nashville: LifeWay Christian Resources, 2012).

CHAPTER 7: MODEL LEADERSHIP DEVELOPMENT FROM THE TOP
1. Leadership Network.
2. Rick Duncan, email message to author, June 15, 2017.

CHAPTER 11: THE PROBLEM OF MISALIGNMENT
1. Used with permission.

CHAPTER 12: ALIGNING YOUR STRUCTURE
1. Ram Charan et al., *The Leadership Pipeline* (San Francisco, CA: Jossey-Bass, 2011).
2. For more on the relationship between Mahler and Charan, see the following articles: "From Loading Dock to CEO in 6 Painful Steps. Or, Navigating the Leadership Pipeline," WordPress (blog), January 9, 2009, https://frrl.wordpress.com/2009/01/09/from-loading-dock-to-ceo-in-6-painful-steps-or-navigating-the-leadership-pipeline/; Stephen J. Drotter and Ram Charan, "Building Leaders at Every Level: A Leadership Pipeline," *Ivey Business Journal*, May/June 2001, https://iveybusinessjournal.com/publication/building-leaders-at-every-level-a-leadership-pipeline/.

CHAPTER 16: AN UNDEFINED SYSTEM . . .
1. Steven Kryger, "Why You Need Systems to Grow a Church,"

Communicate Jesus, January 20, 2012, http://www.communicatejesus
.com/why-you-need-systems-to-grow-a-church/.

CHAPTER 25: CHOOSE YOUR LEADERSHIP COMPETENCIES
1. Email April 25, 2018.
2. Tanner Turley, email to author.

About the Author

Mac has a passion for developing leaders, especially in the area of church planting. He is a graduate of Moody Bible Institute (1984) and Dallas Theological Seminary (1990). In 1997, he planted Carolina Forest Community Church (Myrtle Beach, South Carolina). In 2004, he began serving as Leadership Development Pastor at Seacoast Church (Charleston, South Carolina) where he served for over six years. In 2011 Mac worked with Brian Bloye to start the LAUNCH Church Planting Network. After five years Mac and Brian gave the North American Mission Board the church planting system they developed. Mac went on to serve as the senior director of Church Planting Development for NAMB's Send Network. Today he does church consulting full-time helping churches develop intentional leadership development strategies. Mac and his wife, Cindy, live in Charleston, South Carolina.

Follow Mac on his blog and on YouTube
www.maclakeonline.com
www.youtube.com/maclake.